"It's a rare thing to find a book that seamlessly weaves a framework of wisdom, heart, and spirit. "Dream it, Design it, Live it" aligns you with the truth of your soul's desire and intelligently opens the portal to curate your Next Level Life. A seeker's treasure, this book felt like a reconciliation and renewal — The blueprint to become the attuned architect of my best life!"

Andrea Mein DeWitt,
Author of *Name, Claim & Reframe-Your Path to a Well-Lived Life*

"Dream it, Design it, Live it" offers a comprehensive framework to transform your life. Many people struggle with getting past the dreaming stage. Still, author Diana Long helps you explore your innermost desires and provides a practical roadmap to leverage your strengths, articulate your grand visions, and create an actionable plan to accomplish and live them. I have used these strategies for myself and my clients and have witnessed remarkable outcomes. This book is a game-changer if you want to bring your aspirations to life.

Roberto Giannicola
Executive Coach and author of *"You've Got Algorithm, but Can You Dance? — Learn how to lead with heart and empathy."*

Tap into your inner wisdom and intuition and learn how to live Your Next Level Life by manifesting and achieving the dreams that are uniquely yours. Through her 4-step process, Diana Drake Long reminds us all to DREAM BIG! Heartfelt, sparkly, spiritual, evidence based AND practical, "Dream It, Design It, Live It" will change your life. What a gift. I highly recommend.

Gretchen Hydo, Master Coach,
Author of *Break Free From Your Dirty Little Secrets*

"Dream it, Design It, Live It" is the perfect guide to take your life to the next level. Author Diana Drake Long's voice is warm and authentic, and her use of real-life vignettes and examples makes it easy for readers to connect to. Diana offers a unique and accessible process to fulfill your dreams and goals. A clear and welcoming book, this book will be of service to many people! I can imagine multiple audiences. Our world as we know it today will be much helped and energized by this book.

Sarah Flick MD,
Author of *Desire, Mystery and Belonging*

"Dream It, Design It, Live It": The Ultimate Guide to Manifesting Your Next-Level Life is a game-changer for your "next level of life" inspiration and guidance. This book is for anyone on a personal growth path who wants more richness, depth, and texture – more satisfaction and fulfillment in their life and work. Diana helps you identify your innate keys to manifesting your unfolding greatness. What are you waiting for?

Fran Fisher, MCC, Recipient of the International Coaching Federation 2022 *Circle of Distinction* Award, Author of Violet's Vision

For anyone desiring to uplevel their life, "Dream it, Design it, Live it" is the guide you've been looking for. Diana's teachings and real client stories make the guidance both relatable and executable. Get ready for the life you want to live!

Angie Wisdom, Master Certified Coach
Author of "The Non-Negotiable You" / Consultant

"Dream it, Design it, Live It" blends science, stories, and wit to beautifully weave together practical advice for achieving *Your Next Level Life*. Diana walks her talk as she shows us how to identify our big dreams and follow them through. Whether you already have a dream that you think may be unattainable or you have a spark of a dream you want to uncover, Diana shares her proven method for unlocking and achieving it. I highly recommend this book to anyone who is open to being lovingly led through a method that can be surprisingly easy to lean into, and then watching their new life unfold.

Meredith Liepelt, CEO,
Rising Star Publicity, LLC

This book, "Dream It, Design It, Live" It, gives you the permission slip to go after your big dream, and Diana guides you all along the way. In this lively and relatable book, your dreams will take flight, and you are given the tools to get through the adventure and withstand the challenges on the path. It's beautiful!

Ovidiu Grigorescu,
Engineer

DREAM IT
DESIGN IT
LIVE IT

THE ULTIMATE GUIDE TO MANIFESTING
YOUR NEXT-LEVEL LIFE

Diana Drake Long, MS MCC

Published by
Hybrid Global Publishing
333 E 14th Street
#3C
New York, NY 10003

Manufactured in the United States of America, or in the United Kingdom when distributed elsewhere.

Long, Diana.
Dream It, Design It, Live It
     ISBN: 978-1-961757-05-9
     eBook: 978-1-961757-06-6
     LCCN: 2023916349

Cover design by: Julia Kuris
Copyediting by: Wendie Pecharsky
Interior design by: Suba Murugan
Author photo by: Joanne Barratt Photography

Disclaimer : The names of clients have been changed and their storylines have been modified to protect the confidentiality of the individuals.

www.DianaLong.com

Table of Contents

Introduction

"Don't look for your dreams to come true, look to be true to your dreams."

Michael Beckwith

YOU PICKED UP THIS book because you are craving something new and different. Part of you is surprised that you feel this way, and another part is oddly relieved. You think *I wish I could get unstuck*, but you are clueless as to how. Life has gotten stale, and you long for a more fulfilling experience. You want more richness, depth, and texture in your life. Your small, still inner voice is whispering ideas to you when you listen … *"I want to live in Paris"* or *"Wouldn't it be amazing if I could quit this soul-draining job and do something that has impact? It would be great to open an eco-wellness resort!"* You discover that, when you entertain your Next-Level Life idea, you feel a surge of positive energy and feel more alive. Your sparkle, however, is fleeting. Even though you are receiving glimpses of what could be next for you, you also realize that this will require significant changes. It could be where you live, work, or the status of your relationship.

Your inner resistance to making big or small changes keeps you tethered to where you are now. You talk yourself out of your "wild" ideas and snap back to the status quo, where it is safe, comfortable, and familiar. Don't worry; you are not alone!

Dream It, Design It, Live It

It takes courage to choose your dream rather than go down the same well-worn path. It's understandable to want to stay in the known. You may be in the fortunate position of having a life that looks good from the outside, but it simply does not fulfill you. Perhaps you are stuck in a place that long ago lost its appeal, yet you feel glued to it, glumly thinking you don't have any options. The heart wants what it wants. No apologies are necessary.

Consider this your personal invitation to embrace your truth. What would you like to manifest into your Next-Level Life? Grant yourself permission to go after what you want. What you want wants you, too. I believe that to be true. The ideas, tools, and inspiration in the chapters ahead will be your faithful guide to your Next-Level Life. Dreams do come true, and I am excited to show you how to dream it, design it, and live your heart's desires. Life's too short to put up with less than what the deepest part of you yearns for.

My commitment to writing this book became my new dream in my Next-Level Life. I had achieved the dreams I write about in the book that took my life to the next level, and now *Dream It, Design It, Live It: The Guide to Manifesting Your Next-Level Life is* a vibration in that space. As soon as I launched the search for someone to help me, a few detours got in my way. I navigated two heartbreaking losses, but I never stopped thinking about my dream of writing a book. It continued to burn brightly in my heart, and this book is proof that dreams do come true.

Dream It, Design It, Live It: The Guide to Manifesting Your Next-Level Life was born out of my burning desire to change the world, one person, one dream at a time. Each of us has within us a dream that is waiting to be unlocked. You hold the key.

Your dreams are not fluffy and silly. They are how you will fulfill your destiny, weaving together your highest callings, gifts, talents, and skills. People put too much pressure on their dreams as perfect concepts, making them appear unrealistic. Dreams can be big and juicy, but also normalized to be achieved.

For my entire professional career, I have followed this intense desire to understand how to bring forth and ignite the potential within us. I have studied and trained extensively with masters in the fields of personal development, human potential, high performance, and success technology. In the early 2000s, I discovered professional coaching and became an early adopter of this brand-new industry and profession. I currently hold the highest level of credential—Master Certified Coach, MCC, a credential held by the top 4 percent of coaches globally.

I could have gone in any direction with my coaching and accreditations, but I was continually called to teach about dreams and up-leveling your life. When I facilitate a group and talk about these dream concepts and strategies, I watch these ideas take hold of people. A new energy of potential is sparked and amplified by us as a collective. We can see that energy as it is being shared. People are naturally drawn to support one another, becoming instant allies of the dreamer and their dream. I believe we all know, deep down, that if one of us succeeds, we all succeed. It's both inspiring and motivating to witness the collective effect of people taking a stand for their dreams. It is quite the experience to behold the authenticity, integrity, and passion that has been ignited in the room.

Through my personal story and the stories of my clients in this book, I bring decades of research and data to an empowering process designed to make your dream possible. I have curated the content within this book for you, dear reader, with love and intention. My aim is to provide you with the pathway to go after your Big Dreams and give you the tools and strategies you need to confidently step into your Next-Level Life. I have created a simple and effective four-step process to guide you as you achieve your Big Dream. By following these steps, you will be fully supported to take your seedling of a dream to its fullest form.

Once you have clearly defined and articulated your dream, we take it to the design stage and map out the Next-Level Goals of your dream. During the designer stage, you create your customized Dream Blueprint, which becomes your holy grail to reach your Next-Level Life.

I have also included the science behind how to successfully stay the course, no matter what life throws at you. Together, we will address common roadblocks that threaten to derail the dream, and I'll show you how to overcome these obstacles. These skills and tools will serve you for a lifetime.

You'll be introduced to the Dream Catalysts—life-changing strategies to elevate your mindset and amplify positive results in your life. We'll also discuss how to be the best steward of your own "good energy," so you keep your vibration high. You will learn why this is essential for creating a Next-Level Life and beyond. You'll discover that going after your dream is not all hard work but rather a fun ride!

Dream It, Design It, Live It: The Guide to Manifesting Your Next-Level Life is a sacred opportunity for you to honor your dream, and you have in your hands the guide to do so. You may still have scrapes on your knees from falling, or the memories of being waylaid or judged from previous attempts to live out your dream. Imagine if you were given an opportunity to go for those dreams in a different way. I encourage you to put in some time for that possibility.

My book gives you the tools and confidence you will need to make your possibilities a reality. Let me show you how to go for the gold. No more settling for less than what you truly want. Life is too short. I have seen firsthand the magic of what can happen for those who courageously follow their heart, take risks, overcome fears, transform their doubts, and stay accountable and true to their vision for the Next-Level Life. It's breathtaking to behold.

When we follow the callings of our hearts and soul, not only are our lives elevated to the next level, but the world is also better for it.

Clients and participants at my events report that, as a result of working with me, they:

Dream big/Play big
Are more confident and clearer
Tap into their inner wisdom
Trust their intuition
Easily overcome challenges

Understand their way forward

Feel supported with structure and accountability

Feel more gratitude, meaning, joy, and purpose

My clients' dreams coming true include:

Finding their soulmate

Starting a family

Moving to a new state or new country

Starting their own business

Rising to influence in high-level leadership roles

Earned certifications and degrees, including master's and PhDs

Generating more income, far exceeding their expectations

Birthing their creative dreams of writing, art, and music

Dreams do come true. It's hard to do it alone, and the good news is you don't have to.

Let me show you how ... I'm honored to take this journey with you, and I promise to be with you every step of the way.

Dream It, Design It, Live It: The Guide to Manifesting Your Next-Level Life is laid out in three parts. In Part I, Dream It: Envision Your Possibilities, we lay the foundation for the creation of your Next-Level Life by addressing your personal dream energetics, raising the bar, and how to move from your comfort zone. Chapter 1 introduces Dream Energetics, which will support you to elevate the quality of your life, starting now, with strategies to boost energy in your mind, body, and soul. Chapter 2 awakens you with Raise the Bar, helping you see the call of what your heart truly wants and give yourself the permission to go after it. Chapter 3 will create space for you to Leave Your Comfort Zone so that you can have your own "reckoning" by first challenging and then releasing yourself from your current status quo quandary.

Part II, Design It: Four Steps to Your Next-Level Life will support you as you create the scaffolding for the high-rise dream you are building. Chapter 4 guides you in the first step of Build From Strength. You will inventory where you are now with what's working and what's lacking. This will lead you to clarify and name your true wishes for the future. Using this data, you'll create your own vision for your Next-Level Life. You will build from where you are with the second step in Chapter 5, Dare to Dream Big. You'll gather your wishes and assemble them as the building blocks of your dream life. The two primary tools introduced in this chapter are visualization and Dream Vision Boards. Chapter 6 empowers you with step three as you Declare Your Dream. You will advance your Next-Level Life by building on your dream of substance and taking a close look at your internal and outer dialogue. You will learn how to articulate your Next-Level Life vision, become your own dream advocate, *and* enlist allies to support you. In Chapter 7, Be the Architect of Your Dream, you will get into the granular details of step four and take each of the main goals of your dream life and map them out on paper with specificity, resources needed, and estimated timelines, giving you your own Dream Blueprint.

Part III, Live It: Achieve Your Dream Life is dedicated to the fruition of your dream into reality. In Chapter 8, Dream Catalysts teaches you a set of four exercises that will spark your actions and take you to greater heights, faster than you thought was possible. Chapter 9, Overcoming Dream Roadblocks, serves to course correct any of the dream killers that could crop up as you move forward. You will learn effective strategies to overcome fear, insecurity, and self-doubt. In Chapter 10, you will have the opportunity to take inventory again and acknowledge how far you have come in your Next-Level Life. This chapter shares techniques you can use to savor, own, and celebrate the process of your Next-Level Life journey.

The Dream It, Design It, Live It process works! The good news is that this book is evergreen; you can use the process over and over as you continue to evolve your life.

There is wisdom in slowing down first to deliberately increase your life force. Think of it as upgrading your personal operating system. This is the first place we will start with on your dream quest to focus on energy management.

To create a Next-Level Life, you will want to raise your own frequency to support the higher caliber of experiences you desire to usher in. Not only that, expanding your energy reserves helps you to begin living next level right away, sourcing you with positive momentum to manifest your Big Dream. Let's begin. Your Next-Level Life is waiting …

PART I

Dream It: Unlock Your Possibilities

CHAPTER 1

Dream Energetics

"If you want to find the secrets of the Universe, think in terms of energy, frequency, and vibration."

Nikola Tesla

HOW CAN YOU TAKE your life to the next level? I bet you have been thinking about this a lot lately, and I am certain this book will help you find the answer that is right for you.

Does your life radiate your unique authenticity and express your values, wishes, and passions? It's okay if it doesn't. No one has a perfect life. We can all work toward a better life for ourselves and our families.

To reach your Next-Level Life, the first place to start is with your Dream Energetics. Dream Energetics is akin to upgrading your personal operating system. This upgrade provides you with an abundance of energy, a stronger connection to your higher wisdom, and a positive mindset. This inner fine-tuning of your energy management gives you the insights and stamina to persevere with your "dreams come true" journey.

Think of it as an expansion of your consciousness. Using the Dream Energetic tools, you set the stage for your success. You don't have to wait until you achieve your dream come true to live aspects of your Next-Level Life.

With Dream Energetics, you'll start by attending to your body, mind, and soul with self-care practices that catapult you to high personal alignment. We include the totality of you in the equation, not just what your busy mind thinks is a good idea, but also tapping into your intuition through your heart and gut. By listening and nurturing your body, mind, and soul, an alignment happens, and this increased vibrancy translates into tangible results. This is a defining moment.

Dream Energetics opens your eyes and heart to what else is possible.

When striving to visualize a new dream, you can follow the actions that high achievers use to stay in the zone of high growth and potential so that you can also ignite your Dream Energetics and get to your Big Dream faster and easier. There is an art and science to multiply positive outcomes in our lives. To get the life you want, you've got to take exquisite care of the life you have, and that starts with understanding how your three energy centers—your body, mind, and soul—work together to attract your dream to you.

By aligning these three areas of your life, the quality of your daily living will rise exponentially. You will invite in more synchronicity and usher in exciting people, places, and circumstances. This higher level of personal alignment is the key to opening more good fortune. The payoffs are enormous when you have the know-how to increase your vibrational frequency. Your "high vibes" will keep delivering the goods for your Next-Level Life. Think of it as creating a portal to your Next-Level Life that never closes if you remain open and willing to continue to do the work.

The key to manifesting begins with you. You are a multidimensional being, meaning you are not just your mind, body, or spirit. The truth is you don't operate as a silo. All three of these energy centers are interrelated and support your wholeness as a person. When you adopt a lifestyle that honors and integrates your body, mind, and soul, you become more aligned, and it impacts every aspect of your life.

Self-care is not a luxury activity for special occasions; it is an essential success strategy. At the core of self-care activities is an increased connection to yourself. From this "plugged-in" place, your energy is elevated. Everything is interrelated, so creating a high-frequency integration within yourself not only helps you stay motivated and focused as you pursue your dreams, but it also naturally draws you to that which resonates. When you are in a place of inner alignment, you are magnetic and draw things to you as opposed to forcing outcomes and gritting your teeth to accomplish your goals. Life becomes much more magical. Get prepared to experience more synchronicities, increased intuition, and happy surprises.

Here's a peek at how Dream Energetics helped my client Sara set the stage for her success in crafting her Next-Level Life.

Dream It, Design It, Live It

From the outside, it appeared that Sara had a charmed life, yet she was restless and unhappy. She'd climbed the corporate ladder only to discover that when she arrived, her life felt hollow. On paper, it didn't make sense. She had a high-income job, shattered glass ceilings one after another, and become the first woman to lead her department in a large enterprise. Her relationship with her partner was a happy one; she had a nice home, and she could afford the luxuries of life such as designer clothing and exotic vacations. Yet, she would find herself tossing and turning at night, feeling a vague anxiety. She was well on her way to reaching the very top of her profession, yet the stress of the top-down pressure and the unspoken demands to be the person in charge and create the results that others expected of her began to weigh her down. The harder she worked, the emptier she felt.

While this awareness was challenging for my client, I knew that this crisis of confidence about her life was a healthy sign, indicating that change was needed. Sara did not realize it yet, but she was awakening to her inner wisdom. Sure, she could stay on the partner track and earn all the fame and fortune that came with it, but she was coming to understand that she wanted something outside the scope of her current success. This was Sara's dream awakening, the uncomfortable dichotomy of speaking truth to what wasn't working and simultaneously feeling the pull of new possibilities tugging at her. Sara's dreams had changed, yet she wasn't giving herself permission to trust the process.

Sara was a classic overachiever. In our first coaching session, she wanted to get busy designing a new plan for her life, even though she felt clueless about what she truly wanted.

In our coaching, I let her know that the best place to start was her Dream Energetics. Sara was a working Wonder Woman, yet the job had taken its toll on her. She was in a state of overwhelm and constantly pushed herself beyond what was reasonable and sustainable.

At first, Sara was resistant to the concept of managing her energy, and her interpretation of Dream Energetics was relegated to superficial self-care. To her, self-care was a luxury and meant nice (but unnecessary) activities like manicures and blowouts for which she had little time. She had gotten caught up in the intense, take-no-prisoners approach to reaching her goals, with no time for self-connection, self-nurture, or participation in activities that uplifted her mindset and spirit. Sara was missing out on a deeper level of self-care; it was no mystery why she was feeling stuck, lacked inspiration, and had low energy.

Once Sara got on board with what Dream Energetics was and the rationale behind it, she began to prioritize herself in her own life. A few of the high-frequency activities that Sara added to her repertoire included an intentional morning ritual, rekindling a friendship that brought her comfort and laughter, and resuming after-dinner walks with her husband. She also returned to a spiritual practice she had gotten away from.

Within several days of this new way of being, Sara's energy levels began to rise. She shared that she hadn't felt like herself for way too long. She was fueled up, committed to staying with her new body, mind, and soul practices, and she was chomping at the bit to keep going with the Next-Level Life system.

Spoiler alert! Sara successfully followed the Four Steps we will learn about in Part II and was able to boldly step into her Next-Level Life. The truth is that you need to cultivate the highest version of yourself as you build out your Next-Level Life. It is why this chapter is dedicated to Dream Energetics; the secret ingredient that will help you attain the success you desire. For Sara, Dream Energetics helped pave the way for her ultimate success.

Why wait until someday in the future to experience a richer, fuller, and happier life? Igniting your Dream Energetics provides the insight needed to activate your own superpowers with prescriptions for daily practices to keep your energy high, even when times get challenging.

The practices I will show you in all three areas of your mind, body, and soul create a strong and supportive energy that helps carry you forward to your dreams. In contrast, many of us have a mindset that we are the "do-er" and attack our goals at the exclusion of all else. This approach can work in the short term but is not sustainable over time and is certainly not an enjoyable way to live your life!

Good things happen when you are thriving emotionally, physically, and spiritually.

Everything on this planet has energy. Quantum physics reveals that even inert objects, such as the chair you are sitting on, are made of atoms. These atoms have patterns of particle and wave activity. You cannot detect the energy in dense objects (thank goodness, otherwise, you might have a wobbly experience sitting at your desk). But rest assured, if you could see the energy, you would see that there is a defined pattern, oscillating ever so slowly. This energy pattern is imperceptible to your senses, but it is there, nonetheless.

You are an energetic being living on a planet that is composed of energy. Everything has its own frequency. *What does that mean for you?*

Understanding that, yes, each of us is a being that is energetic in nature, including our thoughts and words. Capitalizing on this knowledge, you can take deliberate actions that increase positive energy. The higher your positive energy, the higher your frequency signature, and the higher the correlation to elevated states of consciousness. Dr. Hawkins, the author of several books on energy, has contributed greatly to our understanding of frequency and how it corresponds to levels of consciousness.

So, what's the big deal about having a higher frequency? Alignment occurs when you nurture your body, mind, and soul. Without this higher alignment, over time, your actions start to feel hollow, and your motivation and energy become depleted. This misalignment could mean the difference between achieving, or not achieving your big dream.

From this place of alignment, you enter a state of flow. When you are in a state of flow, your environment seems to bend to your needs. This is where the magic happens. If you think about it, how you feel and how well life is going for you comes back to how aligned and in flow you are. To have alignment and lots of flow in your life, it is vital for you to manage your energy. To get into and sustain a high vibrational state is the conscious practice of incorporating daily self-care activities that nurture energy, uplift you, and keep your energy vibrant. This vibrancy allows you to be receptive to like-minded people, places, and opportunities that align with your dreams.

Let's look at specific ways to create more energy starting with your body.

Body

To generate more positive energy, a good place to start is your relationship with your body. Studies of high achievers reveal a common denominator, which is that high achievers practice healthy habits in the areas of nutrition, exercise, and sleep. Successful people know that their personal energy levels are paramount to sustainable success and have cultivated habits to generate and keep their energy levels high.

None of us is perfect, and it can be easy to fall into some bad self-care habits around the foods you consume. There are some fundamental truths about the quality of the food we ingest. If you eat too much sugar, indulge in high-inflammation foods, load up on unhealthy fats, or use alcohol excessively, it will catch up to you. Of course, you know this intellectually, but it can be easy to fall into a pattern of unhealthy choices to save time, relieve stress, and distract yourself for a minute of pleasure. Unfortunately, that positive benefit you get only lasts, as the saying goes, the moment it passes your lips.

These tasty but terrible habits interfere with your physical and mental well-being and can lend themselves to even more serious health conditions (which are roadblocks to your dream and unnecessary wastes of time and money). Maybe you realize that you have been on a yo-yo diet pattern, spending time on special diets and detoxes to offset the damage you've done, and then falling back into a cycle of eating the same things that make you feel tired and less than sharp and inspired. Going after your Big Dreams is the long game, and you are poised to win it sooner and easier if you take care of yourself as an important priority.

There are so many dietary philosophies and practices out there, and I'm not here to advocate for any of them but rather to bring awareness to you with the purpose of getting you in optimal condition to be ready to receive your dream and stay in the energy of its evolution. It comes back to how aligned you are with your own body to optimize your health and well-being.

Have you ever gone through a detox program that helps reset your health and energy? For many, this might look like the popular Sober January where the choice is made to let go of all the excessive eating and drinking from the recent holiday season. Maybe now is the time to start cleaning and decide to do a green juice cleanse or a sensible diet of protein, lots of veggies, healthy fats, and minimal sugar. To gain more vibrancy and energy, decide to let go of low energy and choose more "high-frequency foods." Your body, mood, and energy will thank you!

Ask these questions:

Do I have plenty of energy?

Do I have a healthy diet?

What unhealthy eating habits do I have that compromise my energy, immunity, focus, mood, or motivation?

Is now a good time for you to explore a dietary reset? If yes, what will you do?

_____

_____

_____

Did you know that physical fitness gives us energy? The science is here, too.

In his book *The Story of the Human Body*, Daniel Lieberman, professor of biological sciences at Harvard, says that exercise is directly linked to increased energy due to the uptick of oxygen throughout the body, an increase of the powerhouse cells called mitochondria (the more mitochondria, the more energy we have; the older we get, the fewer mitochondria we have *unless* we exercise and eat healthier foods) and, finally, regular exercise helps us sleep more deeply, thus restoring our energy.

The good news is that while most of us are not star athletes, we don't need to be. The current recommendation for exercise is 30 minutes per day, averaging 150 minutes per week. There are studies that show that even a "low dose" of exercise of 15 minutes per day has a positive benefit. There's no reason not to do that; all of us can do the bare minimum! Moving your body could look like a spontaneous dance party in the kitchen, pickleball, a walk on the beach, or working out with hand weights. Fold in more physical activity, notice, and make note if your energy has shifted and recharged. The key thing here is getting into the habit of physically moving your body on a day-to-day basis. What you do is entirely up to you!

What is a physical activity that you will implement today? (*Note how you feel after you do it.*

This helps anchor in these behaviors. If it feels good, we are apt to do more of it!)

_____

_____

_____

What accountability structure will you use to implement daily exercise? (*This could look like a Monday-through-Friday noon walk in the neighborhood with a friend or signing up for weekly dance class, etc.*)

_____

_____

_____

Sleep is the third common denominator that successful people share. Seven to nine hours per night are recommended.

Research shows that sleep impacts our ability to regulate our weight and heart rate and better manage stress. Again, this is advice our moms told us, but sometimes, you think you can get away with less sleep. You may be able to pull that off for a while, but over time, a sleep debt is created, which can affect every aspect of your life and your energy, focus, and motivation to pursue your Next-Level Life.

How well do you sleep? Be honest. If you are not consistently sleeping seven to nine hours per night, it's a great idea to look at what is getting in the way. You might benefit from seeing a health practitioner for a consult and/or doing simple tweaks to your sleep hygiene routines, such as eliminating computer screen time right before bed (blue light keeps us awake), turning your bedroom into a calm sanctuary, establishing a wind-down time to ready yourself for sleep, and cutting out heavy meals and/or reducing your caffeine intake.

If your sleep needs improvement, what is one action you will take today?

_____

_____

_____

Our bodies are the vehicles that carry us through life, and it is wise to recognize the value of this level of self-care. By establishing simple healthy habits in the area of nutrition, exercise, and sleep, our energy levels will correspond positively. Join the ranks of highly successful people who know that more energy equals more lifeforce, which equals better opportunities.

Mind

Did you know that people who describe themselves as "happy" are more successful? Is there a way for you to become happier with the side benefit of becoming more successful? Turns out that, yes, based on research done in the field of positive psychology, there are practices you can add to increase your happiness quotient.

Interestingly, the field of psychology and psychiatry used to be exclusively focused on understanding abnormal human behavior and how to treat those with mental health issues. This all has its place, yet there were virtually no studies done to understand the healthy, vibrant, well-adjusted human being until esteemed psychologist Martin Seligman put positive psychology on the map in the early 2000s. This growing branch of psychology has and continues to research the high-functioning individual, looking at what variables contribute to well-adjusted, successful, and happy humans. There is a myriad of interesting research findings from the pioneers in positive psychology that show us the essentials for energizing ourselves for a lifetime of happiness and well-being.

Let's explore how to energize your mental stamina and positive emotions with these three Energy Tools: positive expectations, practicing gratitude, and letting go.

Let's start with positive expectations.

Throughout this book, many of these practices will synergistically work to strengthen your confidence and energize your motivation as you walk toward your Next-Level Life. Here is how to add positive expectations to your toolkit so your actions yield the best possible results. First identify one of your goals that could benefit from a dose of optimism and reframe it. Research shows that if you use your own name, you get an added bump of confidence).

What goal could use more optimism?

_____

_____

_____

_____

What can you say today about that goal? (*Include your name in that statement. Example: Kim, your presentation will be amazing. You've got this.*)

_____

_____

_____

_____

Optimism is defined as hope and confidence about the successful outcome of a future event. Multiple studies have shown that there is a strong correlation between one's positive expectations to a positive outcome.

This may seem like common sense, and it is, and the literature backs it up. It pays to be an optimist and train your brain to think of positive expectations. An optimistic mindset influences all areas of your life, from your health to your goals.

Expect the positive and you will most likely experience it!

Many years ago, I led a weeklong certified coach training in Chicago. What my participants didn't know at the time was that this was the first time I'd led a five-day program. I'd spent weeks preparing, digesting the content well enough to teach it. I'd had a few restless nights leading up to the first day of the training. I was worried that I would not be able to deliver to the level that these people expected and had paid for. It was a big demand, especially for a first-timer with five full days of content to facilitate. I knew that my Dream Energetics were key to being successful, so while I did the hard work of content preparation, I also tended to my body, mind, and spirit to boost my reserves of positive energy. The big day arrived, and for the next five days I gave it my all. It was challenging and rewarding at the same time. The training went beautifully, and I was over the moon with gratitude to have had this opportunity to be a part of this kind of transformative training.

Feeling on top of the world, I woke up the next morning and took a cab to the Magnificent Mile for half a day of window shopping and lunch before I caught my flight home. After playing with cosmetics in Saks and trying on some shoes in

Nordstrom, I worked up an appetite and spotted a perfect place for lunch: The Peninsula Hotel.

As I walked into the lobby, the beauty of the décor blew me away. Huge, gorgeous displays of live flowers, crystal chandeliers, and gold everywhere; it was a feast for the senses. As I paused to take all of this in, I asked myself, *How does it get better than this?*

This was when the famous rock star Rod Stewart and I almost collided head-on. I was beside myself with delight at this surprise encounter. Once I gathered my wits, I realized that this magical moment came about because A) I was in a magnetic state of being, and B) I was open to even more "goodness." When you expect good to come into your life, it will because you invite it in. The question is: Are you in a high-frequency state and do you hold the expectation and receptivity that something good is coming your way?

The next Energy Tool is the power of gratitude. The results of practicing gratitude are astonishing, and it is one of the most easily integrated exercises you can add to your daily routine. Research with thousands and thousands of participants has shown that a simple exercise of acknowledging three things we are grateful for, done once a day for a minimum of one week, creates significant results. People described that they felt greater well-being, less stress, happier, and more motivated.

Gratitude grounds you to what is happening *now* (not the past, not the future, but right here, right now). Your list of three things to show gratitude for can be anything, from eating a delicious ice cream cone to the warmth of a puppy snuggling with you as you watch TV to a song you heard to a meal someone prepared for you to a sunset to the grace of being forgiven for a mistake you made to the moonbeams streaming through your bedroom window. Big or small, please make a note of how you feel after adopting this practice for a at least one week. Chances are you will want to keep this up indefinitely!

The Gratitude Practice

Every day for at least a week, acknowledge what you are grateful for. Reflect on three good things that happened to you that day and write down what you are grateful for and why. A good time to do this is right after dinner or a few minutes before you go to sleep.

What are you grateful for and why?

1. _____

_____

_____

2. _____

_____

_____

3. _____

_____

_____

Letting Go

Another way to gain more mental energy is by letting go, especially of the past. A lot of us hold on to memories and emotions that are no longer useful in our lives. When you periodically do a "cleanse" and clear out what is outdated, it provides space for better things to come in. If you want to invite your Next-Level Life in, do you have room for it?

Letting go is a fabulous way to create more space for your truest priorities and get busy deleting what is taking up space and dragging your energy down. Maybe your house needs an edit, such as organizing a messy garage or tackling an overstuffed closet. Or it may be emotional or mental clutter, such as holding on to disappointments, frustrations, and sadness from past relationships.

You may wonder how cleaning up your closet or letting go of your attachment to a past relationship has anything to do with your Next-Level Life. I'm here to tell you that holding on to these outdated aspects of your life is heavy and weighs your energy down. These items take your precious energy and clog up the field that could be used to call in elements of your dream. Make a concerted effort to make peace with your past and let go of what you no longer need. Notice the lightness and freedom that you get from releasing the old. Think of how you felt the last time you did some spring cleaning. It's like waves of energy come rolling in once the old is cleared out.

What is an area in your life that you could "clean up" and let go of what no longer serves you? (*Think: old emotions, outgrown relationships, overstuffed closets, etc. Be sure to make note of how you feel after you do this! Anchor it!*

_____

_____

_____

Soul

Connecting to your soul is not just how you discover your callings for your dream, but how you keep your dream alive in a deeper way. Each of us has our own inner connection to a higher source of wisdom. In our busy days, this connection can get lost as you deal with the constant demands of your life.

To hear what your soul is saying to you requires you to be still, present, and listen. I will share with you two potent Energy Tools to raise your level of soul connection: cultivating your intuition and nature's gift. Both are deeply gratifying practices that will bring you many insights, more peace, and increased creativity as you lean into your Next-Level Life.

Cultivating Your Intuition

To follow your dream, it's a critical component to be able to trust your intuition and know how it shows up. Most people are operating without a conscious connection to their intuition. The secret is to provide a space for it. Not only will your intuition begin to show itself to you, but you'll also notice that you receive flashes of insight throughout your day. When you are working in a state of spirit, whether it is intentionally or through your everyday life, you get good ideas that are non-contestable. They show up in a myriad of ways. Some of us "see it," or have a premonition or a vivid dream, others hear an idea or message, and others are kinesthetic—we get goosebumps or waves of energy through our body when we are "on to something." The key is knowing how your intuition shows up (as a primary, like an inner knowing, or a secondary, which could be a dream), and learning how to evaluate and trust it. The invitation is to build your intuition muscles by paying attention to how you get your messages and have the courage to follow those pings.

As I committed to becoming more present to myself and my environment, I began to trust my intuition more and more. I often wake up in the morning with an idea or an answer to a problem. I also learned over time to pay attention to my body's reactions.

How do you receive your intuition? Do you trust it?

_____

_____

_____

Do you feel confident in its guidance or are you 50/50 on the validity of the information?

_____

_____

_____

When you are achieving a dream, you are not in a linear space, and there will be variables that you have never experienced. Fear can show up, and it's essential to tap into the signals you can receive from within to power through to the other side.

Now you are looking to be in the zone with day-to-day infusions of connection. Your spiritual connection is personal to you and continual. For some, it may mean a daily forest bathing excursion; for others, praying or reading inspirational books or listening to music that lifts one up, and/or all the above. There truly is no one right way or one-size-fits-all approach. Besides making the space and time for this kind of connection, be in the essence of presence wherever you are. To be fully present doesn't require a special meditation cushion, it simply requires you to be more conscious and live in the present moment.

When Gandhi was asked how he had the time to meditate while he was working on the colossal project of world peace, he was quoted as saying, "How can I not? Because I have so much to do, I will meditate for two hours instead of my one hour." Gandhi knew and taught the value of spiritual connection and how it can support navigating the material world.

Nature's Gift

Another profound way to create more positive energy is by participating in nature. Science shows us that spending time in nature impacts our physical well-being, mental and emotional states, and is the perfect conduit for us to connect in a deeper way to our higher selves. Many people have some of their best epiphanies and thoughts in nature away from their phones, emails, and other forms of distractions.

There are many ways to participate in nature. The place to start is by identifying what your favorite nature spots are and what is nearby. Maybe you love the mountains and live in Colorado, so you put hikes into your calendar so that you have a steady diet of nature. If you are an ocean lover and can walk on the beach, make space for that in your weekly schedule. If you are in the city, search out your favorite parks and find a way to integrate "green space" into your day-to-day life. Initially, your logical mind might tell you that you don't have time for this luxury. This is simply not true. A few minutes of being in nature pays big dividends that you can feel immediately.

"Earthing" or grounding, is another way in which we connect with the energy of the earth. It's as if the earth transfers its positive energy to us via the electrical exchange that occurs when you walk barefoot on the grass or sand. This brings you health benefits, such as more energy, reduced stress and inflammation, and better sleep to name a few. Earthing is one of the safest and most natural things you can do to improve your well-being. It doesn't cost a dime and requires no special shoes or equipment. Just you and the earth for a few minutes each day. It's nature's gift.

Another way to energize yourself is by taking a walk in a natural environment, often called "forest bathing." This practice is as old as time, but the specific practice originated in Japan, where it is called Shinrin-yoku. The research is clear, as the benefits of this direct and conscious connection with nature are

numerous, including more energy, increased focus and awareness, better relationships, increased immunity, reduced stress
and anxiety, and the list goes on. Common sense tells us it does
feel good to be outdoors, but science shows us to how great an
extent this is true.

The question is: Do you include nature into your daily
life? Likely not. Maybe you have fallen into the mindset of
designating this kind of enjoyment (extra credit and benefits
if you go barefoot!) to a weekend if you are lucky to have
scheduled the time. I would counter this thinking with an
invitation to incorporate walks in nature multiple times a
week if not every day. Your energy will respond favorably!
With more energy, more things are available to us. It's like
having a secret key to unlocking greater success toward creating your Next-Level Life.
Based on what you've learned here, what is your new commitment to enjoy nature?

_____

_____

_____

Try each of the exercises and see which ones resonate with
you. Rotate the ones you choose to do and give each a chance to
raise your vibration. The way you get to your desired outcomes
is by staying the course and energetically being a vibratory
match for your dream. You can do this daily, lifting yourself
up with these various activities that elevate your energy and, in

turn, up the velocity of your frequency. As you keep elevating, magic happens.

The magnitude of setting a dream in motion is that it will open the door for something bigger and better than you can imagine. This is the "secret sauce" to how you keep your dream alive in a deeper way.

Congratulations! You have opened the portal to your Next-Level Life, and with your commitment to your daily alignment practices, it will bring that dream to life faster and easier than you can imagine. Welcome to your new life!

CHAPTER 2

Raise the Bar

"As we let our own light shine, we unconsciously give other people permission to do the same."

Marianne Williamson

MY SENSE IS THAT you are a person on the path of personal development, and you've created success by taking deliberate actions to have whatever "the next" is for you. For many high achievers, success happens almost automatically, but they don't spend a lot of time thinking about what their motivation is. They move fast, set big goals, and conquer them consistently until, one day, they wake up and can feel that something is missing or just feels off. Life's been good, but … it's time for a change. They have an understanding that their current way of living isn't cutting it any longer. *Oh crap!*

Being in this space where you feel ready for the next move but are not sure what that is can feel daunting. You've come this far, you've had many successes, yet it's like you've come up against a wall and aren't sure how to go beyond it. Somewhere along the way, you stopped thinking there were more dreams to be had, which couldn't be farther from the truth. You get to create new dreams every day. Will they all be attainable? Possibly not, but you can always stretch your wings.

The exciting truth is that you have the right to live authentically for you and no one else. You don't have to live other people's agendas or do what you think you "should do" versus what is truly in your heart. This is 100 percent true, yet I know personally how challenging this can be. Your Big Dream may be a million miles away from your current situation. For many of us, it can feel as if it is impossible.

Living the life of your dreams can appear to be complicated, sometimes impossible, to achieve, but it does not have to be. Through my teachings and experiences, I will lead you, step by step, to what I call your Next-Level Life. The process I teach is not the old-school, hard-core method of accomplishing goals, no more pushing and forcing outcomes with sheer will and extreme effort.

The truth is that the old way of getting things done is a lot of work. Shiny goals can look and sound good, but if they are not aligned with your personal values, you may reach high levels of success but feel discontent upon achievement. Often this discontent is met with more striving and goal-setting, creating a hamster wheel effect. Then you feel misguided, often by yourself, and disheartened. So, you go back to pushing and striving, hoping it has a different outcome next time.

Chasing success without consulting our heart's desire is the difference between what I call a "dry" goal and a "soul" goal. Dry goals are those goals we pursue because our head thinks we should versus a *soul goal* that is informed by your heart's wishes. When the head is in control and isn't in communication with what our heart truly desires, the results may look good on paper but will eventually fall apart. The pursuit to achieve is often based on what you "should" do and is not rooted in the truth of what you really and truly want.

The head usually doesn't know! It's good at making plans and executing, but it isn't where your inspiration lies. This is such a limited approach and it's a sad one, too. I've met many people who chose a career path or partnership for all the wrong reasons, even though, to the outside world, it looked like a great life choice.

A common underlying motivation for life choices is connected to money. Many people equate making a lot of money to happiness and let this notion drive the choices they make. Researchers at Purdue University found in a large analysis of over 1.7 million people in 164 countries that the "happiness set point" and its connection to income level is around $75,000 per year. Research shows that our level of happiness and sense of well-being does not increase dramatically as our income increases.

Money is important, as it's the currency we use to provide a living for ourselves, yet there is a limit to how much we need. The study indicates that once our basic needs are amply met, this is achieved at an income level of around the $75,000 mark. More money doesn't necessarily mean more happiness and fulfillment.

Another study done at Princeton University found that there are tiny incremental increases in happiness as income goes up after the baseline of $75,000 to $95,000. However, this was not the total picture. Individuals who pursued increasing their income, thinking it would make them happier, did not experience that result. Those who equate income with happiness are generally less happy.

The reason I share these research findings is that many people use money as their motivation and reason to make life choices. If money were taken out of the picture, many would choose differently. Life satisfaction is more than the money and is more directly influenced by pursuing higher and more meaningful goals. Many people chase the money but discover they are more miserable than they ever were. They are seeking a sense of freedom but have not identified their personal definition of what this means to them. There is no one-size-fits-all definition of success.

When you are living your Next-Level Life, your sweet spot with success is deeply personal and unique to you. The common denominator to true success is when you can freely choose what and where you invest or spend your time, energy, and financial currency in the way that lights you up and gives your life depth, meaning, and fulfillment. As the previous studies show us, money is not the direct connect to happiness and fulfillment, yet many of us follow the money as our North Star instead of our own inner compass.

Maybe you feel held in place with "golden handcuffs." You never imagined that where you are in your life would no longer make you happy, but now you are craving a new freedom. When you entertain the idea of making a big change, it feels a bit overwhelming. You know that making a big shift doesn't just affect you, but would impact those in your bubble, such as your family and friends. There is a real risk that you may be judged for your decisions. The opinions you receive from others can be potent, and their projection of their concerns or fears upon you can cause you to second-guess your choices. It can be a solo and somewhat lonely road without the support and positive reinforcement from our loved ones. Taking a stand for what you know is right for you, especially when your decision impacts other people as well, takes courage.

Raising the bar isn't for the faint of heart. My client Claire came to coaching with the intention of reinventing her life. She was in the throes of an unexpected and contentious divorce and attempting to co-parent their teenager, who was reacting to the divorce with great difficulty. To add more to Claire's plate during all this personal drama, both of her parents began to experience failing health and required her time and attention. As her family's major source of income, she also felt stuck in a corporate job that had lost its appeal. Her job provided ample income but left her exhausted and unsatisfied. She revealed that her secret wish was to leave corporate and start a new business. She was vulnerable and overwhelmed about the current status of her life but was also willing and courageous. She said she was ready to take her life to the next level.

We started with Claire's Dream Energetics. She was physically, emotionally, and spiritually depleted. Her first coaching assignments from me had Claire increase her personal energy reserves in all three areas—body, mind, and soul. With revitalizing self-care practices in place, Claire's energy levels increased. Now she had the stamina and mindset required to navigate family difficulties with grace and grit. Despite family and friends who were concerned about her choices and changes, she stayed true to herself and carried on living with authenticity. She left the corporate gig to begin her new life as a full-time artist. She has had remarkable success with her unique and modern artwork, which, as of this writing, is on display in galleries all over Colorado. As a result of her dedication to the process, she triumphantly stepped into her Next-Level Life. Like a phoenix rising from the ashes, step by step, Claire rewrote the narrative of her life into the story she wanted to live.

To truly start to ascend into your Next-Level Life, the secret is to begin living your next level today by adding in specific activities that boost your energy.

I speak a lot about energy with my clients. It's critical to address our physical, emotional, mental, and spiritual reserves of energy. It's the equivalent of money in the bank. If you want to make a big purchase, you have the collateral to make it happen. In the next step of the Next-Level Life process, you will learn how to combine energetic dynamics, exercises, tools, and the steps to synergistically give momentum to your Next-Level Life.

My Story

The Four Steps to Your Next-Level Life were birthed after an experience I had at a women's networking event in New York

City. The icebreaker activity our leader facilitated was called *Claim Your Desires*. We were instructed to partner up and take turns sharing our wildest dreams and desires. Sounds like that would be fun and interesting, right? You know what happened? Overwhelmingly, this group of successful professional women (more than 300 of us) fell flat. It was crickets in that room. For a few long and awkward minutes, many women struggled to access anything juicy. No dreams. No excitement. Just women looking at each other, feeling stuck, not knowing how to answer the question: *What is my deep desire?*

I was one of those women stunned into silence who didn't know how to answer the question. As I faced the woman who was my partner for the day, I was a deer in the headlights as much as she was. *What are my desires?* I didn't know. My partner waited, expecting my response. There was an empty space there. I didn't have answers. I hadn't a clue how to answer that question.

I scanned the room and noticed that not everyone was stuck. There were pockets in the room where the animated conversations were taking place. Their positive energy was contagious and sparked new possibilities for the one who shared and the one who listened. Like the famous movie scene in *When Harry Met Sally*, I wanted to have what they were having!

I knew what some of my goals were, but when challenged to declare what I really wanted, I froze. You see, I wasn't telling the dream I had deep inside because it appeared so out of reach. My dream was to live in San Diego, but I thought the possibility was completely out of the question. So, I tucked that dream away in the deep freezer, not letting it see the light of day, no matter what.

I left that event a changed person. I knew there was more to life than living on autopilot, which many of us fall into. I committed to honoring my dream even though it seemed impossible to achieve.

For many of us, our dreams are like hidden treasures. They are within us but may be hiding from our active awareness. The book you hold in your hand is your treasure map to your Next-Level Life.

Let's first define what a Next-Level Life looks like:

Next-Level Living is a natural byproduct of being a human on this planet! Our DNA is deeply encoded not only to survive but to evolve as human beings. It is inherent in each of us to learn, grow, and transform. Just as the acorn seed is imprinted with the intelligence to become the mighty oak, each of us has our own unique intelligence to become all that we can be. Your potential is far beyond what you can possibly imagine.

At the heart of every Next-Level Life dream is a draw from deep within to:
Be authentic as our true self.
Be fully self-expressed in our own unique ways.
Live a life that is resonant with our core values.
Have the freedom to choose and act on our higher callings.

There is not a straight line to evolution. Evolution is a process and, sometimes, you hit plateaus and feel like you are stuck.

This is perfectly normal. Some of us may stay stuck longer than we'd like but know that evolution is on your side. Change is inevitable and even more empowering when you choose it for yourself.

Perhaps you sense that you may have outgrown your current circumstances. What once made sense or seemed right now no longer fits. This can be a hard thing to admit. You may see that some of your choices in the recent past have been in response to community, work, family, or cultural expectations. I have worked with many clients who were shaken to discover that their current circumstances were not a true match for who they are and what they truly wanted.

As clients hear themselves talk out loud and reveal the raw truth about what is missing or what no longer fits, it brings up emotions. As you become more awake to what you are tolerating or settling for in your life, there's a tiny crack of possibility that also becomes evident. This opening pulls you to go toward it. Deep inside, you recognize that you are being invited to take a bigger leap toward having a more fulfilling life experience. The variety of emotions that bubble up to the surface when you are at this place of awakening can include feelings of frustration, discontent, restlessness and irritability, excitement, anticipation, and hope. There's an inner realization that you've been treading the waters of your life too long, going through the motions in your life instead of diving into deeper waters and feeling inspired and on point.

How do we take our lives to the next level?

Let's take a tiny speck of an idea that you might be holding. When you consider this new idea, it seems outlandish, unrealistic, and untimely. But, as luck would have it, you may have noticed that this idea has "legs," meaning it doesn't just disappear. This is the sprout of the desire that will become the dream that you will work through in the Four Steps. You notice it pops up in your awareness from time to time, perhaps by presenting itself to you in a dream or during a shower or while on a walk. Creatives call this kind of communication "the muse," and the muse serves you by supplying you with novel ideas to pay attention to and perhaps pursue. The muse is present in the pursuit of Next-Level Living.

What do you do when the muse comes to you with a new idea or a better way to do something? Do you welcome it, or do you brush the gift aside? Are you willing to consider what the muse is showing you? Is it possible that you are receiving information about the components of your Next-Level Life? I would offer to you, yes, this is exactly what is happening, and congratulations are in order!

The default behavior is to quickly brush the idea aside as if to say to this impulse, "Not now. Can't you see how busy I am?" As you stay awake to the two voices speaking to you, your muse and your inner critic, you can feel the push and pull of the opposing forces. No wonder it's hard to make a move. But know this—you have opened the Next-Level Life gateway. You are primed for change, and your Next-Level Life is waiting in the wings for you. What you want wants you.

When you have an important next-level dream, part of the process is to honor the dream, however impossible or outlandish it may seem to us. Take writing this book. Even though the goal of writing a book seemed important to me, it was always on perpetual hold. Life kept getting in the way. The truth is that I wasn't being honest about what I truly wanted and to make it a priority. A lot of us get caught up in the "how" of what it would take to make the dream a reality, and it seems so "out there" that we take the path of least resistance. We just sigh and let it drift back to the back burner.

In this part of creating our Next-Level Life, it is not the time to get too analytical and beat yourself over the head with the question "How will I do this?" and prematurely conclude it's too far out of reach.

One of my clients, Michael, used to say, "Get the how out of here," and I loved that concept. There is a time and place for strategy, but when you are in the dreaming phase of creation, your best practice is to court your muse. Pay attention to your new ideas and notice how your energy feels. If your energy feels uplifted, light, and excited, you know that you've got something worth paying closer attention to.

It's time to take the back burner dream and move it front and center!

The hard truth is that if you aren't living your highest and best versions of yourself, you are not aligned to your personal integrity. Being out of personal integrity with ourselves is uncomfortable and painful. It's like having a pebble in your shoe, but you pretend it isn't there, walking with it in there, tolerating it. The weight of not truly living the life you want and resigning yourself to accept that certain goals are out of our reach is a hidden/secret burden that many of us carry, and it creates a lot of internal stress.

Stress is stress, and when you aren't attending to the root cause of your stress, the stress will not disappear but accumulate and grow stronger over time. This can look like getting derailed by an unexpected illness or accident that makes us stop, take pause, and reset. I would like you to find your next dream in an easier, softer, less painful way.

It's much easier on us to make the decision to choose what you want versus having to go through a traumatic/dramatic event that forces your hand to make different choices than what you have been doing.

Either way that brought you to this book, whether it's an event that is requiring you to make a big change or that you are following your inner guidance and deciding that this is the time, I am happy that you are here.

Change is at hand, and it also provokes most of us to want to hunker down and keep things "safe" and comfortable. It's okay if you don't know what you want yet, or perhaps when I asked you to identify your passion, it scared the pants off you. Know that this is a normal reaction to change. You just don't know how to take this big, daunting dream into real life.

I will be with you all the way with a process that helps make the unseen known and defined, and will get you into life-designer mode. Once you create momentum, it's just a matter of time before you put your Big Dream into motion and your Next-Level Life begins to materialize in real time.

To be where you are in life today, you've likely done your fair share of personal development work such as therapy, workshops, and self-help reading. This was time well spent by you; it's helped you to clear the way to arrive at higher and higher levels of your own life's creation. At the same time, it can feel daunting to think, *Here I go again. I am going to have to "push" myself to get the results I dream of with this seemingly impossible goal. Do I have the time, energy, and stamina to pull this off, especially with everything else that is on my plate?*

As you start to gaze at what's possible for you next inside, you find not just the dream, but its soul …

How do you know that you've tapped into a dream that has soul?

It's thrilling. When you think of it, it feels exhilarating and brings a smile to your heart.

It's meaningful to you. It's connected to your values.

It feels daunting and may feel impossible to achieve.

These are three distinct signs that you are on the right track with your Big Dream.

The formula to achieve that next Big Dream: Dream Energetics and the Four Steps to a Next-Level Life are based on these soul goals as well as facing your deepest desires. Fortunately for me, my desire to have a place on the West Coast didn't diminish over time. The "muse" kept calling to me with signs, coincidences, and ideas about what it would be like to take this leap. I used Dream Energetics and the Four Steps that I share in this book with you to manifest this unlikely outcome of calling San Diego my home. The process was not linear or obvious, but over time, I saw paths open. It all began with the inner awakening that life was calling for a change. As crazy as it seemed at the time, I had the willingness to leave my comfort zone.

As normal as it is to brush away a crazy, random idea that seems to come out of nowhere, it's critical that you nurture those seedlings of desires and pay attention to the messages they give you. If you could truly have what you wanted in the next chapter of your life, what would it be?

Together, let's find out.

CHAPTER 3

Leave Your Comfort Zone

"The privilege of a lifetime is to become truly who you are."

Carl Jung

IMAGINE A NEST of cute baby robins, all cozy and tucked into their safe little space with Mom and Dad caring for their every need. A sweet image. Until one day ... Mama bird coaxes each bird to leave the nest. Quite the unexpected shock for the baby bird, but nature knows best.

Staying in the nest isn't a viable option for those robins, nor is it for you! You may have been getting the signs for a while that it's time to leave the cozy nest of your current situation and fly on, but you hesitate because you do not know what you want yet. So, you stay, and stay, and stay ... until one day, you've stayed too long.

Your Next-Level Life is new territory that is just beyond the horizon of where you currently are. You may intellectually understand this, but you may not yet recognize when it's time for a change. You've reached the pivot point.

Before we launch into the four-step process, let's examine some clues that you are ready for this work. Pivot points are powerful, and they are exactly that—points in time that signal that you are ready to make a shift. The clues that you're ready for a pivot can include feelings of irritability, resentment, or boredom. The irony is that even though you have a vague awareness that you are feeling less than enthusiastic about life, and you notice that you are just going through the motions, the common response is to hang on to what you have because, let's face it, even though our "comfortable" situation isn't really all that comfortable anymore, it is familiar. I call this the "coasting phase." The coasting phase is akin to driving a car as you head down a small hill. It's easy to take your foot off the brakes and let go of the steering wheel for a short time. Yet, if you steer your life like this for too long, the farther you can drift away from your "true north."

Coasting is seductive because it allows us to hang out where you are, feel safe, and be immune from taking a risk. It has many faces. It could look like your sister complaining of her unhappy marriage (for years) or the person who is disengaged at work but isn't proactive to change the trajectory of their career, or the friend of yours who has spent the last year talking up the brilliant idea that she has for a startup, but she's stalled and takes zero action.

Mariana came to me during her version of the coasting phase. She was frustrated with her career and, as she stated, nonexistent private life. She was going on 12 years as a teacher in a public school system in a metropolitan city. Up until this year, Mariana had a strong work ethic, evidenced by the extra time she gave preparing the curriculum and teaching her popular classes. In addition, she filled her days with tutoring, chairing multiple committees, and as a volunteer advocate for teachers' rights in the school district. Her love and passion for teaching had, however, lost its luster.

Mariana was no longer enthusiastic, and she began to coast at work, doing only the bare minimum to get by. Coasting gave her space to conserve some of her energy, but she knew she couldn't coast indefinitely. She was stuck with no Plan B in sight.

Mariana was hard on herself, unhappy that she let this all go on for too long. She began to realize that she had ignored many signs that she was not resonating with her career.

One day, the internal pressure came to a head. Mariana reached her pivot point, determined to find the way to create a new life for herself. She wanted to play a bigger, bolder game. She was ready to stop coasting, grab the wheel, and direct her life onto a more fulfilling and meaningful path.

For most of us, we keep coasting until, one day, we reach a pivot point and something inside us says, "I need to make a change. Period. The time is now."

Frankly, this pivot point doesn't magically come with all the answers yet, but you are tuned into the inner realization that it's time to create a new chapter in your life story. It usually happens without fanfare. You find yourself waking up one morning and the "jig" is up; you just cannot deny how you feel. Finally, you tell your own truth. You are not happy in your marriage and know there is a better aligned love for you out there. Or your job doesn't see your value, and you know there is a place of employment that will. Perhaps where you live is too congested, and you crave silence. It may be one big thing or several parts of your life that need a reset. You may not have the answers, but you know it's time for a fresh new path to open. It's perfectly normal to know it's time for change yet not be clear on what the specifics are.

High achievers, by nature, are energized by projects and plans and they are skilled at making things happen.

To be in the space of the pivot point is unsettling for most people who like to have the answers and be actively working on the solutions. It's not an easy place to be, especially for high achievers. Within the pivot point is the tiny seed of the dream you have been ignoring or repressing, like the voice that told me San Diego was home and I chose to ignore it for so long.

Psychologists call this scenario of the unknown of your dream holding the tension of the opposites, meaning you are actively straddling both of your worlds—the world in which you are still in and the urge to create a new world. When you can allow the tension of these opposites to co-exist without fighting it, this will generate new possibilities more easily and quickly. Holding the tension of the opposites is uncomfortable but well worth doing. Two things can be true at the same time, you may be at your endpoint with some aspect of your personal or work life, AND you can actively explore what is next, even though you may not know what that is. That's okay!

In order to create a Next-Level Life, it will require you to let go of areas you have outgrown yet are all too familiar and comfortable. It takes courage to break free from your own version of the status quo.

Wanting to be in control of our life, we often go to great lengths to keep our life neatly inside the border of our comfort zone. Routines in daily life provide a sense of comfort and safety, and who doesn't like that feeling? Yet, there are some routines that will quickly become a rut that you justify. This could be a habit, such as the guilty pleasure of watching TV with your laptop in bed three nights a week and defend doing it because you work hard and need to unwind. In the back of your mind, there is a nagging feeling you are wasting time. That is your pivot point.

Let's take this comfort zone idea to another level with the status of your entire vocation. Say you are not in love with your current role at work, but the thought of making a change is too overwhelming. Instead, you tell yourself, *this job is not that great, but at least I know what I am dealing with versus having to feel the discomfort that comes along with making a big change in my life, such as quitting my job and striking out on my own with the gluten-free bakery business idea I've been daydreaming about for a couple of years.* Your internal dialogue goes something like this, *I just need to stick it out, keep my head down, and work hard so that I keep rising up the ladder and make more money. Then maybe I can go for my Big Dream of what I really want.* This strategy looks good on paper but robs you of your heart's truest priority.

Instead of waiting it out for a better time, a more ideal scenario, or having more money in the bank, perhaps life is asking you to be brave and authentic. Is now the time to be honest about what you want to change?

Changing the status quo into something brand-new requires both passion and perseverance.

Research conducted by Angela Duckworth, PhD, and author of *Grit,* found that achieving success is positively correlated to two factors: passion and perseverance. We've all heard that if you follow your passion, the money will follow and sayings to this effect. Dr. Duckworth's research pokes holes in this idea. Passion alone is not enough. You must also have the willingness to do the hard stuff' that comes along with your desired outcome. When you set a new target with your dream goal, you may experience setbacks, distractions, and have difficulty staying focused. When you have both aspects of passion and perseverance operating, which Dr. Duckworth calls grit, you then have leverage to accomplish your goals and create your Next-Level Life. To raise the bar in your life, you will need to draw upon both your passion and perseverance. In other words, to be "gritty." The end results will be your Next-Level Life.

Through thousands of hours of coaching sessions with clients, I see this common pattern—people who, with the best of intentions, cram commitments of every kind into their lives. Their lives are, without doubt, full lives, but not a life they are fully living as they continue to yet deny themselves from stepping into the dreams they secretly hold in their hearts. It's as if you are under a spell where constantly moving is the norm. You are a master of the to-do list, but passion is missing. In order to create the next level, you need both passion and perseverance.

Take a moment to reflect, to sink into your deeper knowing. Take a few nice, natural, deep breaths, close your eyes, and answer honestly from your heart space:

What is a dream that you are passionate about creating next?

(This question helps you drill down to your truth about what makes you feel alive. We are all creators! Are you a closeted artist, creating paintings or jewelry in your spare time? Do you obsessively watch travel shows because you secretly yearn to live in a different country? Are you a weekend chef and dream of becoming your version of the next Julia Child?)

Write down your answer(s) here:

_____

_____

_____

Are you willing to do what it takes to bring your passions to their fullest expression?

(This question is also a dose of truth serum. By owning what makes you come fully alive, you mentally and emotionally take a step forward. You recognize that your passion is like oxygen—you must have it in your life to stay alive. This brings you to a choice point. Are you willing to take your

life to the next level by honoring your daydream and give it a chance to be a dream come true?)

Write your answer here:

_____

_____

_____

The comfort zone can be a trap. If you stay glued to where you are and coast indefinitely, you no longer feel the healthy tension of being challenged. Life will start to feel like you are on a hamster wheel, going round and round but not feeling like you are going anywhere interesting.

We humans are a funny bunch. We say we want change, but when it comes down to making the change, we stall, hoping for a miracle to happen so we don't have to make the new or hard choice.

My client Amira is a talented graphic designer with an impressive resume, working for major corporations all over the globe. She recently married and had two children. Her life is a beautiful one, yet there was one area that no longer felt like it fit. She felt the inner tug to start her own company and scale it. She had confidence that she had the talent and the resume to prove it, but marketing her own services was brand-new territory for her. Amira was used to showing up, doing her magic, and getting paid well. To scale her business to the level she envisioned would require Amira to overcome this marketing hurdle to attract the quantity and caliber of clients she wanted. To make this all work, Amira needed a solid marketing and promotional strategy. This was a big leap for her.

She was a self-identified introvert, so marketing was not her cup of tea, yet she needed to start sipping from this teacup if she wanted to bring her Next-Level Life into being. She could stay in the safety of her current comfort zone or break free and create her own successful business. She chose to break free.

It takes guts to change, especially when the current situation you have created for yourself is enviable. You may have a life that others wish for. There is a collective tendency toward sameness in our culture. Doing things out of the norm, being creative, thinking outside the box, and taking risks are not embraced with open arms by much of our culture, including our family and friends. It's as if we have an overprotective mom who wants us to stay safe by being careful and not taking risks. But the biggest risk in life we can take is ignoring our dreams and keeping everything in status-quo mode.

In *Regrets of the Dying*, documented by Bonnie Ware, people who were close to death stated that among their biggest regrets were wishing they'd had the courage to live a life true to themself instead of the life others expected of them, and wishing they'd let themself be happier. What wisdom.

Getting to this pivot point is usually a bumpy road at first. It's a courageous act to own the dissatisfaction you feel and to embrace your emotions as an ally. Your emotions are signaling for you to pay attention and they wake you up from sleepy status-quo mode and invite self-awareness. By embracing your "uncomfortable" emotions as signposts guiding you to a new future, you can bravely explore what new possibilities you want to create next.

Some of us hold on to whatever we've created for dear life, even when it's clear that we aren't happy with it. It seems easier in the short term to keep things humming along as per usual. We may put on a happy face, and grin and bear it.

My client Mae Lin was so afraid to fail at new endeavors and strike out on her own in her career that she kept making excuses to stay on in a work environment that she had long outgrown. Her cultural background was a strong silent influence. Mae Lin had been taught to value hard work to the exclusion of a personal life. Primary role models in her life implicitly messaged, "Don't make waves," and be loyal to your employer. She was overqualified for the role she held.

Every day had a sameness to it, yet it was familiar and "comfortable," so she kept up a lie to herself that she needed to stay put and wait until the timing was right. She'd secretly argue with the two parts of herself. The one part that was scared to change would tell her she shouldn't rock the boat and it wasn't worth the risk to change jobs now. The other voice that spoke from her heart was boldly whispering to her to go for it and that it was time for a change, life is short, and enjoy your life and your work. For what seemed like an eternity, she toggled back and forth, asking herself: *Should I stay, or should I go?* In order to have a Next-Level Life, she would have to face her fear of risk and break free from the constraints that no longer fit. Anais Nin's beautiful quote comes to mind as I share Mae Lin's dilemma with you.

"And the day came when the risk to remain tight in a bud was more painful than the risk it took to blossom."

Mae Lin chose to bloom. What about you?

There is a dream inside you waiting to be expressed. Maybe it's starting your own business, such as a gluten-free bakery, or to attract your soulmate, or become the CEO of a Fortune 500 company, but your dream is kept hidden by the spell of the comfort zone.

The comfort zone seductively keeps you in place, despite what you tolerate. The voice in your head says it's too hard to change. I need more time. The truth is things won't change until you do. The potential discomfort of making this choice keeps you stuck right where you are. For now.

Underneath the noise of the comfort zone lies another voice, the voice of your intuition. Intuition is defined as your ability to unconsciously process a person or situation without facts or mental deliberation. You "know" something without additional information, analysis, or discussion. The concept of intuition can seem irrational, especially when you typically use facts and metrics to make decisions. Intuition is the product of the rapid unconscious processing of previous experiences and patterns that instantly crystalize into a conscious "knowing."

Psychologists call this a "thin slice" perception. You encounter a situation that you intuitively get a "hunch" about, such as sensing danger or how trustworthy someone is.

Some scientists can use what they "sense" to guide their path forward to make potential discoveries. Michael S. Brown, geneticist and 1985 Nobel Prize winner, was quoted as saying, "As we did our work, I think we almost felt at times there was a hand guiding us." This brilliant Nobel laureate was instrumental in groundbreaking discoveries that positively impacted the field of medicine and treatment protocols for decades to come.

You have access to this inner guidance ... if you listen closely and pay attention.

So, how do you know the information you are receiving about your Next-Level Life is your intuition talking to you? What we know about intuition is that it is a skill we can cultivate and is worth doing! One of the best ways to optimize your intuition is to pay close attention to how you receive your intuitive "hunches." You can utilize and trust your intuition more effectively when you actively note when and how the intuition comes to you.

There are four main ways in which you can receive your intuition: auditory, visual, kinesthetic, and deep knowing. People who are auditory will tend to process how something sounds to them, and their intuition may come as a message they hear or react to what they have heard. A visual person will go with how something looks and may receive their intuition through a dream or a vision of what could be, or some other visual sign in their environment. Kinesthetic people will have a physical component they feel, such as goosebumps or a feeling like a wave of energy running through their body when they encounter a person, place, or concept they are considering. A deep, confident knowing that your intuitive hunch feels completely true for you is an amalgamation of all three. Each of us has a primary and a close secondary way of receiving our intuition.

The Intuition Game

If you want to learn how to trust yourself more, an excellent exercise to use is the Intuition Game.

For 21 days, pay attention to and note when and how you receive intuition. Jot down your discoveries in a notebook. What you focus on helps your brain to mark the moment. After 21 days of paying attention to your intuition, what patterns did you notice? How do you receive your "hits?" Is it primarily through visual, auditory, kinesthetic, or just plain "knowing" what you know? By marking these moments and noticing how you receive your intuition, you increase your brain's connection and recognition of intuition and how it appears to you. The more connected you are with our own intuitive signals, the more you can lean into it and trust it.

Your intuition is your inner cheerleader, nudging you awake so you can notice what feels off in your life and often gives you a glimpse of what is possible. The problem is that you might not listen, or you get busy and forget the nudge you received. Fortunately, intuition doesn't give up. It may whisper in your ear, come as a visual, or give you waves or tingles, or a knowing deep down in your bones. But have no fear! Even if you keep tuning it out, it will get louder and more obvious to you.

For example, with my client who would stretch out of her comfort zone by building her bakery brand, she learned to trust her intuitive hits more and noticed that signals from her environment picked up pace. As a result of being more present and aware, she experienced more synchronicities—signs and happy coincidences that mirrored her dream. These signs served to strengthen her confidence, affirming she was on the right path and empowering her to act toward her dream.

Unless you learn to trust your intuition and check in with your heart or gut, you are apt to keep doing what you've been doing. Honor the message your intuition is giving to you even if you don't fully understand it yet. Track these intuitive "hits," notice what energizes you or what feels heavy. These clues can lead us to a creative breakthrough instead of a wake-up call that could have come in a gentler way.

When it comes to decision-making, the inner challenge is: Are you up to make a move and tolerate the risk? It is especially tricky when your life looks good from the outside looking in. The problem with staying in status-quo mode and not challenging yourself to reach for more, keeps you stuck, frustrated, and in denial, and, over time, could develop into drama and trauma, such as an unexpected divorce, financial woes, or serious illness. These more intense life experiences force your hand, requiring you to make changes that you have ignored for too long.

Instead of passively staying in your predictable lifestyle, secretly wishing for something different, you can be proactive and partner with the creative, generative force—the universe. Why not become an ally with the universe, take charge of your life, and make choices intentionally versus letting "fate" determine what happens to you?

While life can, and does, sometimes bring us huge obstacles to overcome, this is not the only way to create breakthroughs in your life. You can spark your own breakthroughs without having to deal with trauma and drama to get there!

I invite you to believe in and commit to the power and beauty of your dreams, to take your life to the next level. I also encourage you to stop worrying that you don't have permission to want more and to get out of the mindset of "I should just be satisfied." If you are not, you are not, and you can get to the bottom of what holds you back. This book will be your catalyst and "pocket coach."

I admit that leaving your comfort zone isn't easy to do at first. But I promise you, as you begin the process, it will free you to create a Next-Level Life. As we partner together in the Next-Level Life process, each of the Four Steps will allow you to pave the way organically and intentionally for a more beautiful life. I am a big believer that life supports you when you show up for yourself. The fact that you are holding this book, reading this at this moment, is significant, and I am right here with you to support you in the creation of your Next-Level Life. Ready? Let's activate your Next-Level Life by taking the first of the Four Steps, Build From Strength.

Dream It, Design It, Live It

Here is the pathway to your Next-Level Life. In the following chapters, we will go through each of the Four Steps to Next-Level Living, and I will walk with you all along the way.

PART II

Design It: Four Steps to Your Next-Level Life

CHAPTER 4

Step One: Build From Strength

"Happiness is the consequence of personal effort. You have to participate relentlessly in the manifestations of your own blessings."

Elizabeth Gilbert

I **'M EXCITED FOR YOU!** You have completed the initial phases of Dream Energetics, Raise the Bar, and Leave Your Comfort Zone, and now we can take the first step on the pathway to your Next-Level Life.

The pathway will take you on a journey through Four Steps to pave your way to a shiny new future. Let's begin with the first step, Build From Strength. This step will give you a clear accounting of where you are currently. You will know exactly where you stand, including the "good, the bad, and the ugly," and I promise you this information will serve you well.

You may be thinking, *let's get on with it, let's jump ahead and get my new plan into place.* But that's just it, taking the time to see clearly and accurately what your current status is will become the material we will use to build out your Next-Level Life. With step one, you will discover and understand what isn't in alignment for you and transform it into higher, better versions worthy of your Next-Level Life.

Let's begin.

When you spell out what is not working in your life, it's as if you just took the pressure off a valve that was about to blow. It takes a lot of energy to keep these tolerations, such as complaints, unhappiness, and frustrations, just below the surface. By reviewing where you stand with 12 specific areas of your life—**Money, Health, Career, Spirituality, Physical Environment, Fun and Adventure, Growth and Learning, Creativity, Significant Other, Family, Friendship and Community**—you will quickly get an accurate accounting of how your life measures up for you.

No one loves making a list of their complaints and aggravations but let me explain the method behind this madness.

Imagine that you are in a swimming pool and trying to keep a beach ball completely submerged under the water. You are able keep the ball underwater for a while but discover it takes a lot of your energy to keep it there. Eventually, that ball is going to pop up to the surface.

When you actually let these "negatives" float to the top of the water where you can see them and feel what they are about, you are now in a place of more conscious awareness. When you have awareness, you can stop living on autopilot.

These three exercises will guide you in shifting your life from one that runs on autopilot to a life where you make intentional choices at every stage and in every area of your life.

Build From Strength has three exercises:

Life Check-In – Exercise 1 is where you check in with the 12 main areas in your life and assess ratings.

Tolerations Audit – Now that you have your ratings from your Life Check-In, in exercise 2, you define what is not optimal and what you are tolerating.

The Wish List – In exercise 3, you transform your tolerations into your Wish List for your Next-Level Life.

Life Check-In

If you are like many people, reflecting and checking in on the quality of your life may not be something that you do on a regular basis. For a lot of people, New Year's Eve is the closest they come to reclaiming their desires for a better year and setting audacious goals. Every December 31st, all over the world, with their champagne glasses raised in a toast, people share their new, barely hatched New Year's resolutions.

While making champagne-infused declarations can feel exciting, most of us don't really believe in the new resolutions we just made, and, within days or weeks into the new year, those resolutions are abandoned and forgotten. In fact, Richard Wiseman, professor at the University of Herefordshire, conducted the New Year's Resolution Project in 2007, which tracked over 3,000 people who set New Year's resolutions and were determined to achieve those goals. One year later, the study determined that 88 percent of people fail to accomplish their resolutions within 12 months of declaring them.

A similar study conducted at the University of Scranton by JC Norcross and DJ Vangarelli in 1988, found that while 77 percent of individuals maintained their commitment for a week, that number fell off dramatically within months. Two years later, only 19 percent had succeeded, with the remaining 81 percent failing and their resolutions all but forgotten. By utilizing the three exercises in Build From Strength, you will get a leg up on your success with your own goals. The distinction is to set goals with clear intentions so that your Next-Level Life goals are specific, measurable, achievable, realistic, and time-based.

Exercise 1 is where you check in on each of the 12 main areas in your life and assess ratings.

As you begin the Life Check-In exercise, I encourage you to give yourself the gift of uninterrupted time and set yourself up for success. Grab a mug of coffee or cup of tea and settle in for powerful and effective truth-telling. Be sure to have a journal handy (you will want to take notes) as we move through this process.

Take the 12 aspects of your life listed below and simply reflect on each category. How do each of these areas measure up for you? For example, are you off-the-charts happy with how things are going in the money arena or is it lacking in some way? Is your physical health excellent or are there some issues that calibrate it to a lower rating? Deliberately go through each of these categories and assess the rating you would give this part of your life today.

Be straight with yourself. This is not a time to sugarcoat how you perceive this part of your life. We want the real and raw truth. Be completely honest. Avoid excuses, justifications, or any other analysis. Just go for the truth as you see it, clean and simple. How do each of these areas in your life measure up for you? What rating do you give each part of your life?

The results you get from doing this Life Check-In will be uniquely yours. No one has a perfect life. There always are and will be opportunities to grow. This audit helps us to see where those opportunities are.

Next to each category, rate on a scale of 1-10 (a rating of 1 would indicate you aren't experiencing fulfillment in this area of your life; conversely, a rating of a 10 would indicate that you are "rocking" this part of your life and are satisfied).

Money
Health
Career
Spirituality
Physical Environment
Fun and Adventure
Growth and Learning
Creativity
Significant Other
Family
Friendship and Community

This audit is simple to perform yet can bring up mixed emotions. Areas that you rated highly boost your mood. It feels good to acknowledge what is working well for us. Areas you have rated lower may bring up your frustration, fears, or worry to the surface … just like that beach ball we try so hard to submerge under the water.

When you take an honest look at your life, you'll discover in which areas of your life you're excelling and in which parts you feel fulfilled and happy. Again, what a wonderful confirmation.

We can leave these areas be for the time being.

Then there will also be areas you wouldn't rate highly, and as you score that for yourself, it brings awareness to where you've been hiding or ignoring signals that you are far from where you want to be.

On a scale of 1-10 (1 being low and 10 being the highest level of satisfaction), let's say that you scored yourself a 6 with money. It's neither super low nor super high in terms of your happiness factor. Here is where we can do a deeper dive:

What is bothering you about the money you make?

What doesn't work anymore for you financially that may have worked a few years ago?

Just as we go through developmental stages from birth to old age, our purpose and potential have growth stages. Who you were and what you were doing 10 years ago, five years ago, one year ago, or last week is going to be different from today and your aspirations for tomorrow, next year, and beyond. Your life is begging you to get on with it!

What is the next level? This process sparks a fresh, new conversation with yourself.

Another way to do this audit is to draw a circle on a piece of paper and divide it into equal wedges as if it were a pie. Each wedge represents one section of your life, such as finances, career, love life, family, etc. Now shade in each pie wedge to the percentage of satisfaction. If you scored your finances with an 8, then shade in 80 percent of that wedge. Do this for all the pieces of your "pie." Once you have done this, you will have a visual representation of your life.

If you took this pie with its different wedges shaded in, you'd have an odd-looking, irregular shape. Maybe some of your pie wedges are completely shaded in, others hardly at all. It's a mixed-up pie. Once you can identify the specific areas that you want and need to change and name the items that are not working for you to up-level, you've got a recipe for dreaming big.

The Life Check-In exercise helps you to take your own temperature and shows you where life is stellar and where it falls short, and can reveal what is missing, frustrating, painful, or boring. It also reveals where you may be doing relatively well in a particular area. Let's say you rated the friendship category as an 8. Just because it's not a 10 doesn't mean that you must take this on as one of your goals. It's simply good information to know. You get to choose what you want to focus on.

When my client Adrian came to me, he recognized it was time to move past his comfort zone to shape his new future. The Life Check-In exercise was instrumental in helping him quickly identify the three areas that he scored the lowest— Career, Money, and Environment. He now could address those areas specifically. The lightbulb turned on, shedding light on aspects of his life that he deemed were no longer acceptable and bringing into focus what he truly wanted. Adrian was keen to be part of an organization whose vision, mission, and values would be 100 percent aligned with his. He had specific financial targets he was shooting for. He was also motivated to relocate his residence, even though he hadn't figured out any of the logistics yet.

Adrian also had a fourth area, Significant Others, that he scored lowest of all, but he wasn't keen on working on it. In our discussion, he told me the reason he scored this area so low was because he didn't currently have a significant other, nor was he actively pursuing dating. He was interested in finding a partner someday, but this simply was not the time. He decided to channel his energy toward his top three goals to create his Next-Level Life.

When you do your own Life Check-In and evaluate your scores, choose your true priorities. Even if a score is low and your truth is that it's not your current priority, that's fine. What are the areas that inspire you and you are motivated to tackle? The exercise shines the spotlight on your current reality—the good, the bad, and the not-so-great. By measuring each of these vital areas of life, such as your money situation or your relationships, you can tap into the discontent you feel in that part of your life.

When you stop and acknowledge that something is off, whether it be subtle or downright obvious, something shifts deep within you. It's hard to pretend that everything is "fine" and keep carrying on with your life when you have this inner awareness. I wish I could tell you that this beginning phase of your Next-Level Life is a piece of cake. It's not easy for most of us!

It's tempting to gloss over this new awareness by pulling back from the truth. You may be tempted to fall into old habits to distract yourself, such as putting your head down to navigate a never-ending to-do list or getting lost in social media streams. In the short term, this does make you feel better, although it's a temporary fix. Being willing to look at what is really happening (or not happening) in your life gives you the opening to zero in with a magnifying glass and identify clearly what is misaligned.

Sometimes the Life Check-In creates an unconscious resistance, and you may rationalize that things aren't so bad, so you decide to remain where you are because what you have uncovered feels overwhelming. Don't worry; this happens to most of us! Maybe it feels scary to look at it, or you tell yourself you don't have the time or money for it, or you just don't know how to change it, or maybe you are so used to it being this way that you've resigned yourself that this is how it will always be. You pile on the justification, reasons, and excuses as to why things are the way they are, but you still feel it … like you want to ignore that giant beach ball that is floating right in front of you, or you're tempted to grab it and push it back under the water. But let's be truthful; you know it's going to come back up to the surface. Are you brave enough to accept it so that you can change your circumstances? I hope you say yes!

Now, let's turn up the heat and tell your hidden secrets, all the places in your life you are pretending that "everything is fine" but really isn't. I call this the Tolerations Game, and we all play it.

Tolerations Audit

Now it's your turn to name all the tolerations you are enduring. Go full out with this part of the Tolerations Audit exercise. We'll start by taking a frank look at your 12 ratings. Of those 12, which is the top priority for you? Second priority? Select up to three main areas for this part of the exercise. This is important. You don't want to attempt to change every single aspect of your life all at once. The best way to do this is to choose a focus and go up to a maximum of three main areas to highlight. There is no wrong or right in terms of what you choose as your main priorities.

The Tolerations Audit exercise is a catalyst for you to open your eyes and take ownership of what is not to your liking. Bringing attention to these tolerations will change your life!

Living your life in default mode can work for a while but isn't sustainable or desirable for long periods of time, let alone our entire lives.

The results you get from doing this Tolerations Audit will be uniquely yours. No one has a perfect life, and there are always opportunities to grow. This audit helps us to see where those opportunities are. To spark your heart's desires, goals, visions, and dreams, look at each of these categories and write down what you currently have there that you don't want. Allow yourself to brainstorm. *What am I tolerating?*

At first, you might think nothing much … *My life reflects what I want it to be.* However, I invite you to pause here to take a closer look and reflect. You will discover that there are indeed aspects in your life that you are tolerating, putting up with, or have simply gotten complacent with. Tolerations can run the gamut, from small, seemingly unimportant items to big, life-changing circumstances.

You must acknowledge your current reality and take full responsibility for it. You must be honest with yourself before you can move forward. From this point of contrast, you can see clearly what is working and what is not in your current life choices and environments. Whatever you are tolerating, whether big or small, becomes the precise information needed to springboard into the deep waters of your biggest dreams. This data provides the way for you to articulate what you want to do, have, feel, and experience in your Next-Level Life.

A useful version of this exercise is to make a running tolerations list for a couple of weeks then begin handling those tolerations one by one. The Tolerations Audit often begins as a daunting exercise, but I assure you the amount of energy that you will free up will astound and delight you. Start with the tiny tolerations, handle them, and you'll immediately feel the benefit of freeing up more space in yourself. This free space equates to more viable energy that you can use toward more fulfilling goals that help to shape your Next-Level Life.

An interesting phenomenon I see over and over in coaching sessions is the answer that a client gives when asked the question "What do you want?" Most people answer this question by describing what is not going well in their life. That's normal. We tend to hyperfocus on what is right in front of us, inhibiting our ability to envision what we would really desire. The way to create the next level is to take the time to name and delete old patterns and circumstances so they can be transformed. Doing this will shed light on what is going on; what works, what doesn't.

This exercise is liberating and sets the stage for transforming these tolerations into the seeds for a richer life, a life rich with purpose, meaning, contribution, joy, fun, prosperity, adventure, and more.

For example, let's revisit my client Adrian's top three priorities. His ratings were as follows:

Career – 5
Money – 6
Physical Environment – 4

From here, Adrian brainstormed all the tolerations he could think of for each of these three areas and wrote them down.

Career Tolerations

I don't have the autonomy to make high-level decisions.
I have stayed longer in this role than I should have.
I put up with the misalignment of my values by staying with this company.
I earn okay money, but it could be much better with my skill set.

Money Tolerations

I should stop renting and invest in purchasing a home.
I spend a lot of money and save or invest little.

I really want to break the 350k mark for yearly income.

I don't make time to understand how to generate more income, including digital investments.

Physical Environment Tolerations

I've lived in my hometown all my life and have not explored anywhere new.

My condo is okay, but not my dream version of a home.

My furniture and decor have no theme, lots of hand-me-downs, and dated pieces that are not my style, worn out, or just look sad.

It takes almost an hour to drive to the airport, and I travel a lot for work.

There's a lack of cultural events or diversity in the town I live in.

Once Adrian named the tolerations for each of his three areas of focus, he was able to use that information to formulate what he truly wanted. His set of tolerations became transformed into his preferences and became his official Wish List (which we will do next).

Now it's your turn to engage your inner alchemist and turn what's less than desirable into the gold you long for:

Focus Area #1
Toleration:

_____

Toleration:

_____

Toleration:

_____

Toleration:

_____

Focus Area #2
Toleration:

_____

Toleration:

_____

Toleration:

_____

Focus Area #3
Toleration:

_____

Toleration:

_____

Toleration:

Transforming Tolerations into The Wish List (Setting Intentions)

Here's what Adrian's tolerations transformed into:

Career Tolerations

I don't have the autonomy to make high-level decisions.

Transformed into

I want to be in the executive-level management at a forward-thinking company.

I have stayed longer in this role than I should have.

Transformed into

I want to find my next-level dream job.

I put up with the misalignment of my values by staying with this company.

Transformed into

I want to work with a company that is led with the highest of integrity.

I earn okay money, but it could be much better with my skill set.

Transformed into

I am sought after for my skill set and earn money commensurate with this level of expertise.

Money Tolerations

I should stop renting and invest in purchasing a home.

Transformed into

I buy my dream home.

I spend a lot of money and save or invest little.

Transformed into

I revamp my entire money management system and earn and keep more money than I ever have.

I am embarrassed about my nonexistent investment portfolio and earning far less than I should.

Transformed into

I break the 350k mark for yearly income in my new job's paycheck. I find ways to create multiple streams of income.

I don't have time to understand how to generate more income.

Transformed into

I become well-versed and act on alternative investment opportunities and create wealth beyond my wildest imagination.

Physical Environment Tolerations

I've lived in my hometown all of my life and not explored anywhere new.

Transformed into

I research and visit places that I'd like to live in and find my perfect new city.

My condo is okay, but not what I want now to be.

Transformed into

I start looking for my dream home in my ideal location.

My furniture and decor have no theme, lots of hand-me-downs, and dated pieces that are old broken, or just look sad.

Transformed into

I let go of the old stuff I don't like and purchase furniture that reflects my modern/clean style.

It takes me almost an hour to drive to the airport and I travel a lot for work.

Transformed into

I live within 25 minutes of a large airport.

I am so bored with where I live; there is a stark absence of cultural events and little diversity.

Transformed into

I live in my ideal location, which is multicultural and offers a steady flow of events that fulfill my creativity and entertainment needs.

Adrian was in high gear after completing these three exercises and, with his newly defined Wish List, he was able to identify one Big Dream and moved onto the next step in the four-step formula toward his Next-Level Life.

Now it's your turn to transform your tolerations into your Wish List

Toleration transforms into: _____

Toleration transforms into: _____

Toleration transforms into: _____

Repeat this with every toleration you have for your three main focuses.

When you look at your Wish List, what emotions does it bring up for you? Excitement? Doubt? Both?

Our wishes help us see where we have split energies. It is exciting to generate a new Wish List and, at the same time, it's tempting to go into our mental mode and get granular about logistics and quickly feel overwhelmed. The inner critic's voice may say, "How on earth do you think this going to happen?" or "There's not enough time or money."

If you are not careful, you will keep yourself stuck in an unfulfilling narrative when your list of complaints and frustrations become embedded in your psyche, as if this is who you are. You start believing the story that you are that person who can never find Mr. Right, or the one who will always have money challenges. You deem these current temporary experiences as if they are etched in stone and that it will always be this way.

Neuroscience tells us that you train the brain with a narrative. This narrative is comprised of memories of experiences and the meanings we make of those experiences. This narrative is based on the past. The brain doesn't challenge it; it accepts it as the current reality. Your reticular activating system is on high alert, scanning your environment for that which provides evidence or matches the narrative. You become your own self-fulfilling prophecy. The way to break this neuro-loop is to transform those old stories into clearly defined intentions.

Here's a quick recap of the process to help keep us moving forward:

Exercise 1: Rate your 12 areas of life from 1-10 and choose your main focuses (up to three areas you want to change).

Exercise 2: Name your Tolerations in each of these three main areas.

Exercise 3: Transform your tolerations into statements of intentions and create your new Wish List.

As you Build From Strength and implement the three phases from the earlier chapters, you are ready to walk directly into Step Two: Dare to Dream Big. This is where things start to get juicy! The time you spend in step one is worth it as it provides the ingredients of your "perfect" life, the specific goals you want to manifest for your Next-Level Life. Let's go there now!

CHAPTER 5

Step Two: Dare to Dream Big

"Authenticity is being true to who you are, even when everyone around you wants you to be someone else."

Michael Jordan

CONGRATULATIONS, YOU HAVE ALREADY made significant progress toward your Next-Level Life by completing Step One: Build from Strength. By being honest with yourself about what's working and what's not working in your life, you've given yourself the gift of clarity. You can see where you have given your power away and you are now attending to yourself and the vital heartbeat of your wishes. Not only that, but by completing the Life Check-In exercise, you've got a snapshot of the top areas that you want to up-level and your own specific Wish List that describes exactly what you want to manifest. Treat this list of wishes like gold because it is!

Your Wish List becomes your guide to clarify your bigger dream. Consider each of those wishes as the building blocks to your new desired future/Next-Level Life.

Instead of letting your inner critic run the show as we unfold this next step, Dare to Dream Big, I suggest you carve out some time to reflect on your Wish List. As you look it over, do so with reverence and what I like to call "soft eyes," meaning you are taking it all in without jumping to assumptions about how it's all going to happen (or not).

By being in a relaxed frame of mind, you can then translate your wishes into intentions that create a vision, setting the stage for a new story in your life that gives you the direction to move to a higher place.

Stories are powerful. When you allow yourself to tell a new story, you click into a higher level of inner conviction and commitment. The old stories you told about your life can keep you stuck where you are, repeating the patterns of your past. You want the new stories reconfigured to empower you to create a new future.

Before we turn your wishes into your new vision, let's first look at some examples of wishes:

> **Meica's wish** is to take her business to 10 times where it is now and make 10 times the money and make 100 times the difference to her customers.
>
> **Michael's wish** is to become financially free by investing in money markets, stocks, or cryptocurrency.
>
> **Lauren's wish** is to meet her soulmate this year.
>
> **Jason desire** is to quit the corporate world and start his own business.

As you review your own unique list of wishes, what are some dreams that scare you or seem unattainable?

Here are some examples you may have put on your list:

I want to be the designer. I don't want to just be a worker in executing the design ideas of others.

I want to create my own screenplay that I then sell the movie rights to, but I've never written a screenplay, and I know no one in the industry.

I want to travel to Scotland to visit my place of ancestry, but I can't find anyone to go with me.

I want to write my own book, but I think I am a terrible writer.

I want to be part of a cutting-edge team that provides tangible solutions for climate change, yet my current job leaves zero time for any extracurriculars, let alone impactful projects.

I want a juicy, sexy, and loving relationship with my partner, but we've been stuck in a rut for a long time.

I want to be recognized globally for my photography, but colossal self-doubt keeps me from taking action.

I want to experience a quantum leap in my personal consciousness and evolution, but I am locked in so tight to my comfort zone and decline opportunities, such as retreats, classes, or mentorship because of my secret fear that I can't handle what I discover.

I wish to compete and win a world-famous ballroom dance competition, but I feel too self-conscious about my body. Plus, I don't have the spare time to take dance lessons.

I wish to live a simple life on a tropical island, writing and painting, yet this seems completely out of the realm of my reality, and so I dismiss the idea.

I wish to live in Italy or France full-time or part-time, but I've only been there on a weeklong vacation years ago, so this idea makes me start thinking I am losing my mind.

I daydream of creating my own unique lifestyle-branded business, but everyone in my world thinks I'm in fantasy land, so I believe them instead of believing in myself.

What each of these wishes has in common is that they are examples of the dichotomy of being out of your comfort zone while at the same time having an undeniable, magnetic pull toward wanting to be fulfilled. It's a heady mix of emotions.

On one hand, you may feel giddy about the possibility, and on the other, it feels impossible to achieve. It's hard to reconcile feeling all these intense emotions at the same time. It can seem crazy that you would consider pursuing these wishes. You second-guess yourself, wondering if you are having some version of a mid-life crisis (no matter what your age), with your inner critic sounding off with one or more of these comebacks:

I'm too busy with my life as it is; how could I possibly add something new? There's no way I have the money to back this dream.

It's too late. That ship has already sailed. I'm too old to start now.

My partner will never agree to this idea.

My kids need me, my spouse needs me, my company needs me, my parents need me, my friends need me.

I don't have time, and it's selfish and silly to daydream like this.

Your inner critic will try to coax you back to "reality," which is exactly where you are right now. If you keep doing what you've always been doing, you'll have the same results you've been having and carry regret into the future until our dying day because you didn't act on your inspirations. What a waste!

Dare to Dream Big and honor your wishes as important, worthy, and possible. You would not even have the idea if there wasn't a part of it that holds potential for you. Whatever your secret wishes are and the inner "noise" that comes along with them, I promise you that your wishes are worth paying attention to, even if you feel overwhelmed by the audacity of them and are clueless about how to accomplish them. Instead of putting these dreams off another day ... at this moment, grant yourself permission to open up the window and let the fresh air of new possibilities fill the room. Notice how the wishes begin to create a new storyline in your imagination. You start to daydream about what it would be like to have this be your new life. Imagine it makes your heart happy and skip a beat with the thrill of the sheer idea. When your wishes affect you in this way, there is no denying it. Don't turn back now. You are well on your way to new adventures.

Now it's time to write your vision.

Your vision is the formulation of your new story into a tangible, believable asset you can propel yourself forward with.

In order to conjure a vision that is fresh and new, I encourage you to think like a painter with a blank canvas. Sink into a creative state. You need a relaxed mind.

Over the years, working with clients and even doing inner work myself, I've observed when you get to this part (translating your Wish List into a vision) resistance often kicks into high gear. While a vision sounds like a good idea, for some reason, you still don't do it! What is going on here?

The phenomenon happens when you resist something you know is good for you. Sometimes you must put on your running shoes and just do it. Or, in this literal scenario, pick up your pen and write your vision. There are no expectations that doing so will make you happy, but once you do it, you will be glad you did. If you are feeling resistance, this is an indication that you need a creative outlet!

Here is my own example:

When I completed my own Life Check-In before realizing my dream to live in San Diego, my top three focuses and wishes were:

Physical Environment Wishes

1. For me and my husband to move to the San Diego area.
2. To find the perfect place to live close to the ocean that fit our budget.
3. To have all the details work out easily and smoothly (including selling our home and figuring out which furniture and belongings to keep or to sell).

Community Wishes

1. To be part of a like-minded community.
2. To find a warm and friendly neighborhood.
3. To find someplace with a good vet nearby.

Lifestyle Wishes

1. To have a yoga studio nearby.
2. To have quick access to beach walks.
3. To have restaurants and grocery stores nearby.

From here, I looked at my Wish List and allowed my imagination to weave the threads together to create my vision for a Next-Level Life. I asked myself: How do I want my life to look and feel? How do the threads come together to create a beautiful new fabric?

Here's what I came up with for my vision:

We find a beautiful place near the sea. Every day, I go to the beach to walk or do some writing or reading. We are so happy. We love our new home. We negotiate a great deal. The neighborhood is welcoming, and we meet new like-minded people as soon as we move in. Our move here is a breeze, fully supported. We have the best help, from selling our house at a higher price point than we ask for to easily choosing what to keep and what to let go of. We make a nice profit and reinvest this money. I am so happy to be near like-minded friends and colleagues and have regular lunch and dinner dates. Shopping is perfect. We have everything we need, from first-rate traditional and alternative health facilities to restaurants, boutiques, entertainment, and groceries. Our older dog adjusts beautifully to the new location, and we find a great vet clinic nearby. We take plenty of weekend trips and explore the West Coast. We have so much fun. My husband finds a gym that he loves, and I do yoga every day. We are excited that we've made this move, and it brings a freshness to our life together. We are living fully, with happiness and new adventures and meeting new people. Our family comes to visit often, and we create many new memories together. Our life here is a dream come true.

And then sealing the vision with the ubiquitous statement …

All of this and/or something even better!

Weaving these wishes together allowed me to organize my wishes into a new story for my life. Notice that this vision is short and sweet. No need to overthink your vision (sometimes that is what keeps us from doing it. We think it's too hard to do or takes a lot of time).

With this new story, I created my vision for my Next-Level Life.

Mind you, at the time, this was all far-fetched and completely out of the realm of reality. There were multiple reasons why this dream of mine made no logical sense. Family was a big one. There was a unspoken family code that said family live close by, no matter what. Living elsewhere was literally a foreign concept. In addition, my husband was happy and successful running his family's brick-and-mortar business. Even so, I trusted in this process of manifesting. I know this four-step formula works, and so I kept my focus on the new story I was telling.

At the time of the birth of this dream, my husband had absolutely no buy-in. With good reason, he thought it was an impossible idea and was set against it. I kept the dream alive within me and did my best to curb the inner critic that kept hounding me, saying, "How the heck am I going to manifest this?" Nothing seemed to line up to support this cross-country migration.

From here, once you have a new script, you can begin to move forward as you now have even more clarity about where you are heading.

Now it's your turn. Take your list of wishes and let your mind's eye take you into your desired future.

Write Your Vision

Use your Wish List as the prompt and brainstorm your perfect life. Ask yourself how you can put together these wishes into a next-level vision of what you want life to be like for you. Grab your journal and, with your list in hand, dust off any old, back-burner dreams and bring them to the front stage.

One of the best ways to tap into your creativity is to provide yourself with an environment that is conducive to no distractions and where you will be almost forced to do the work. Intentionally go to a coffee shop without your laptop. You could sit or go for a walk outside or by a body of water (swimming, showering, or taking a bath works, too). These kinds of settings elicit our creative thinking.

Once landed, grab your notebook so that you can capture your ideas and thoughts. Using your Wish List, look at each of the categories and allow yourself to go deep and wide with each one of them. Explore it and be curious about it. Ask yourself: If I were to be 100 percent honest and had everything I needed to make this happen, what would I really want? Write this down.

Write Your Vision is best done as a work-in-progress writing exercise, spanning over a week of reflection, and capturing your ideas on paper. What is interesting about writing your vision is that you will begin to see how all of your intentions (even if they are in separate categories, such as money or relationships) have interconnections that come together in a unique way as your dream for your Next-Level Life.

Give yourself complete permission to dream big. Really flesh it out on paper without judgment.

If you knew that you could have 100 percent of what you wanted without fail, what shape and form would those dreams take? Are they wild and big like starting a nonprofit to end hunger? Or something as simple as looking fashionable and feeling dynamic in your Zoom meetings? Both dreams are valid dreams and must not be ignored, but both have barriers to entry. Maybe you feel uneducated about the nonprofit sector, so you don't act, and your wardrobe is lacking because you simply can't find time to get Nordstrom. What I find is that these dreams are interconnected because they represent that new level of living and parallel each other. The nicer outfit will make you feel better, and this gives you the extra energy to go for the nonprofit.

Write your vision down in glorious detail. Dive into this exercise with wild abandon, no holding back. No dream is too big to ink onto your piece of paper. It's just paper. Go to town! You are crafting your new Next-Level Life story. It doesn't have to be perfect to be documented, just get started and write it down. Paint the picture of what you would like to experience in your Next-Level Life. Include it all, the tiny and the big details. Include your five senses and the emotions that come up for you.

Journal with an abundant mindset, through the lens of "I cannot fail" and "I have all the resources, including time, money, and support that I would possibly need to achieve this Next-Level Life goal." Once you have documented your vision, challenge yourself even further. What else comes to your mind's eye? What else would you like to experience? Write it all down.

Feel free to add to your vision every so often. The new story you are shaping will continue to morph into concrete manifestations as you move through the four-step formula. Once you have your vision created, you now have a way to "see" it and speak of it. It's no longer a list of items, but a more cohesive vision of where you want your life to head.

Now that you have your vision, what do you do with it?

The first order of action, once you have your vision documented, is to acknowledge yourself for opening a huge portal of possibilities. Well done! Now let's explore how to energize your vision by harnessing the immense power of visual imagery.

What we know from neuroscience research is that our brains are malleable. We can shape our futures by how we "feed" our minds. Imagery is a universal language that directly imprints into our subconscious.

Neuroscience research is fascinating and inspiring. We now know that the neural pathways in the brain are influenced by how you think, act, and feel. Your neural networks are always responding. What you "feed" yourself will become part of your brain's neural network. The more deposits you make (by visualizing, speaking, and taking actions in alignment with a goal) will create denser neural pathways. Knowing this, you must ask yourself: What thoughts and beliefs do I hold about my ability to achieve my big goals? What is the quality of my self-talk? What actions do I take to support or diminish my desires?

Neuroplasticity is directed by repetition and what you hold and believe to be true, whether that be beliefs, stories, or the idea that your past dictates your future. Your brain will continue to loop and keep you stuck in the past.

Your mind is plastic and powerful. When you fuel yourself with positive thoughts and actions, your life will start to change. Change your thoughts, change your life. All that you are today is a direct result of your thoughts, beliefs, and actions.

The first way to Dare to Dream Big and optimize your big-dream vision is to begin to visualize or mentally rehearse your vision. Elite athletes, musicians, and surgeons have successfully utilized this success technology to create breakthrough performances. Michael Phelps, the most successful and decorated Olympian of all time, was mentored to add visualization by his coach, Bill Bowman. You may not be Olympian in training, but you can use this powerful strategy to accomplish the Big Dreams of your Next-Level Life.

In an experiment conducted in 2003 at the Cleveland Clinic, led by Gueng Yue, patients were instructed to conduct imaginary workouts in their minds. After consistent practice, those individuals who practiced the visualization experienced a significant increase in muscle mass, and they hadn't done any physical exercise! The participants gained strength by using their minds. The mind believes what it is being told, and the body responds to it. The power of visualization can do wonders for your future.

So, how do you take this concept of visualization and apply it to your own delicate and new vision?

1. Start with your written version of your vision and let it become your script. Close your eyes and begin to imagine your vision in vivid, colorful, and tactile detail. Infuse your mental imagery with your positive desires and emotional intensity. By deeply immersing yourself in the experience of your vision, you bring into focus the experience of having this vision as real.

2. What does it feel like? Where are you feeling it in your body? Whom are you with? What are they saying to you? What smells do you associate with this vision? What clothing are you wearing? What does this success taste like? What do you notice as you play out this positive scenario in your mind's eye? Play out the full experience of your ideal scenario and pour in your positive emotions and intense desire. See yourself as you wish to be, with all the details of that ideal experience.

3. Repeat this practice of visualizing daily. Set a dedicated time and place to engage your active mind in the details of your vision. Each time you visualize your vision in an intentional place, you strengthen the neural pathways in your brain and create a secondary catalyst for change. This active thought and intentional setting will encourage subconscious thoughts that support your vision.

By practicing a full-immersion visualization like this, you open and integrate the neural pathways associated with the outcomes you desire. You will discover that you will experience synchronicities and new opportunities that will provide you with tangible action steps that lead you to your new life. You'll become more aware of people, places, and resources that are a match to your goals. Visualizations prime your brain to see opportunities that are in alignment with your goals that, up to this point, you just were not aware of. Your body and mind accept the new narrative and you'll discover that you are a "new person" who is led to take actions that align with your desired outcome instead of unconsciously acting out the past.

Years ago, when I was in San Diego to lead a coach certification training, I discovered a beautiful small beach near where I was staying. I was tired from a long week of training, but something pulled me to park my car and go to the beach. The sky was pitch black and illuminated with hundreds of twinkling stars and a gorgeous full moon. I was the only person there.

I was struck by the quiet and the magnificence of this moment and dropped into the sand, laying on my back and gazing up at the spectacular night sky. Something deep inside me prompted me to play out the vision of living in San Diego in the theater of my imagination. What would it look and feel like to live here? To have this lifestyle? To be able to enjoy the sunny days, mild weather, and sandy beaches as part of my every day? It was as if my brain and body registered that moment in time, anchoring it in my dream although it was still far from being realized.

When I returned to the Midwest, I committed to a regular practice of visualizing my San Diego dream. I visualized in lots of different venues—my office chair, my meditation space, my daydreams, but my favorite place was after dark, laying on a blanket in the grass, looking up at the starry night sky. I affectionately called my secret moonlight practice "stargazing in suburbia." I consistently immersed myself in visualizing my life in San Diego, savoring the positive emotions that I experienced on that beautiful beach in Del Mar, and would repeat the affirmation, "Dreams do come true." I surrendered in the trust that it would all come to pass. I did not know how yet, but deep down inside, I believed my dream would materialize.

The key to successful results using visualizing is repetition. David Hamilton, PhD, and an expert in high performance, states in his book *How Your Mind Can Heal Your Body* that the brain structure shifts physically when the visualizer is consistent in the practice of it. The more you do it, the more the brain encodes it. Your brain will believe the stories you tell it.

Here is another incredible true story about the power of visualization.

My client Sergio's primary goal in coaching was to find his soulmate, a partner for life whom he could build a family with. As a personable and social person, he had lots of opportunities to meet new people. He met a woman, they clicked, began dating, and were exclusive for almost a year. Something was off, though. Sergio had come to know within his own heart that, as much as they cared for one another, it wasn't meant to be a long-term relationship. It was a difficult decision to realize this and breaking off the romance was hard on them both.

In a coaching session, what surfaced for Sergio was that he was holding on to some trapped emotions and some limiting beliefs. These clouded his ideas about this past relationship and his potential for meeting his ideal mate. He was ready, willing, and able to go there. In our session, he wanted to work on letting go of the past so that he could make space for his future.

One of the benefits of living near the ocean now is that I can hold "office hours" at the beach. I have a secret place in Del Mar that always seems to have an open park bench overlooking the ocean waves rolling in. We met there for the coaching session.

In this session, Sergio was able to unpack and let go of old beliefs, fully feel his emotions, and was ready to claim what he wished for. I invited him to close his eyes and, in his mind's eye, paint the picture of his ideal relationship in vivid detail, who he was, who she was, what they would connect on and share, and so on.

I noticed, in the corner of my eye, that while my client was rewriting his future in this visualization exercise, a whole wedding ensemble had shown up just yards away from where we were sitting. They were actively arranging the area for an exchange of vows. Within minutes, the flower-studded arch was set up, soft music was floating in the air, and the bride and groom arrived in their beautiful wedding attire, along with their guests.

I could barely contain my awe at what I was witnessing. The exact thing my client was clearing a path for was playing out right in front of us.

As Sergio completed his visualization, he opened his eyes. He had a peaceful look about him.

"I had a huge breakthrough today," he said. "I've let go of what was keeping me stuck, and for the first time, I tapped into what I truly want and what that could feel like." He was inspired and motivated.

I nodded my head, acknowledging what he shared, and then invited him to look at what had transpired while he was doing his "work."

He was speechless. As he had consciously/intentionally created his vision, seeing it like a movie in his mind and anchoring the energy of what he wanted, the Universe showed him his future potential with a version of it in real-time.

It truly was a magical moment and one of the most profound transformations in a coaching session that I've had the privilege to facilitate.

A footnote to this story is that my client continued to practice this potent visualization and meet his "person" shortly after that session. They dated, got engaged, had an elaborate, exotic wedding celebration, and are now the happy and proud parents of twins!

The practice of visualization is indeed powerful. Another way to harness the power of visual imagery is the exercise of using dream vision boards to "out picture" your dreams.

Dream Vision Boards

Vision boards have been made popular in the past decade, but are they effective or just a fun activity? It turns out the answer is both!

Think of the world of advertising. A picture is worth a thousand words. It's no secret that sophisticated marketing strategies are capitalizing on the fact that our brains are impressionable.

We absorb more messaging daily than we realize, with adverts being pushed to us via our smartphones, social media, television, movies, print ads, and so on. Marketers know that repetition is key and send us messaging that gets absorbed by us, often subconsciously. You don't even realize that it's happening. You end up buying products and services that you don't really need or use because you have been heavily influenced by effective marketing strategies.

So, how can you use this science to work for you rather than against you? By curating your own marketing campaign using Dream Vision Boards!

What's fabulous about the Vision-Board process is that it allows you to deliberately and consciously choose imagery that represents how you want to experience your dream goal. Collecting and placing your imagery onto a board that represents your vision inspires and motivates you to achieve the results you aspire to. Consider it the best personal marketing strategy you could be part of, and the good news is you get to choose exactly what you want.

Here's how to create your own Dream Vision Board:

1. **Gather your materials -** Buy a sturdy poster board, scissors, glue sticks, and a giant stack of old magazines.

2. **Light a candle and have a latte** - Turn on music you love, let your imagination and creativity express themselves. Get out of your logical mind and into your fertile creativity zone.

3. **Rules for vision boarding -** Gotcha! There are no rules! Let the images you are attracted to speak to you. Don't edit yourself or your vision. Let the images tell your new story.

4. **Get artsy** - Once you have ample pictures, place your imagery in a pleasing way to you on the board and glue in place.

5. **Display your board -** Showcase your board in your office or bedroom, anywhere that you will see it often and daily. By looking at your finished vision board, you are feeding your subconscious mind these powerful images, bypassing our inner critic who is quick to focus on why or how something can work for us. Let your vision board serve to remind, inspire, and strengthen your neural pathways toward your Next-Level Life!

Another way to create a version of your customized vision board is utilizing Pinterest. Create a private page and begin "pinning" the images that speak to you for your vision. Both versions of the vision board can be added to as you choose, adding more depth and nuance to your visual creation of your ideal Next-Level Life dreams.

Using both methods of visioning (practicing visualization and creating a vision board) will absolutely strengthen your dreams. Using this methodology allows you to bypass your inner critic. It is a powerful way to anchor the vision into your being so that you believe it and act on it.

I encourage all my clients to use the tool of dream vision boards to build and broaden their visions. I've had the pleasure of clients sending me a picture of their incredibly diverse vision boards, and I love to use this tool at the end of the year. It's great as a solo project but also lends itself to a fun girls' night or weekend family experience.

Over the years, I have offered my Dream Big in-person events, which have empowered participants to discover and unlock the door to their Next-Level Life. Attendees were from a wide variety of industries and life experiences, ranging from attorneys to financial advisors, engineers, graphic designers, to physicians. They all came with their own unique twist of what their Next-Level Life could be.

Several years ago, at one of my Dream Big events, hosted at a historic hotel ballroom in Worthington, Ohio, the main activity was a guided opportunity for the participants to create their own vision boards. The vision board exercise is a powerful way to access one's clarity about what you value most, the dreams and goals you have, and then assemble a visual collage of it. Attendees were from diverse backgrounds, and each had their own unique reason to attend this type of event.

Susan was drawn to come to the event because she was at a crossroads in her marriage. Tien was searching for more meaning and purpose in her work life. Brandon wanted more life balance with a goal to scale his business and still have time at home with his partner and children. Emma was looking for a spark of inspiration, as her corporate career was no longer fulfilling, and she was confused about what to do next.

Once I set the stage for the participants about how to get started, the room quickly filled with the positive energies of potential and possibility, with lively music playing in the background. They collected colorful markers, looked through magazines, and selected pictures and quotes to artfully compose their visions onto poster board masterpieces.

Everyone in the room let their imaginations take flight. High-level leaders cut loose and got into a playful and creative space as they sifted and collected images that depicted the essence of their dreams and goals. They went from the overused logical brain that they use daily in their profession to a creative and resourceful space. Once they had their images collected, participants arranged them into a beautiful collage on posterboards. After the vision boards had been assembled, the pure joy in that room was palpable.

Checking in with those workshop attendees a few months after the event, the vast majority had exciting news to share about what had transpired in their life since that workshop. Those images that held the "message" of their visions were coming true. Here are a few of them ...

Alana's dream? She had begun writing her memoir.

Ron's dream? To leave his corporate job and start his own consulting business.

Mitchell's dream? To get back in better physical shape, joined a runner's club, and, six months later, ran his first race of many what?

Pamela's dream? She went back to school to finish her degree.

Amber's dream? To open up a yoga studio called The Wonder Within.

When you incorporate your visualization practice and vision boards, you will strengthen your dreams, allowing you to bypass your inner critic. It is a powerful way to anchor the vision into your being and bring it into the world!

In Dare to Dream Big, you crystalized what your vision can be, and you now have two easy and enjoyable ways to anchor your dreams. This cues us up to the Step Three: Declare Your Dream.

CHAPTER 6

Step Three: Declare Your Dream

"Authenticity means erasing the gap between what you firmly believe inside and what you reveal to the outside world."

Adam Grant

NOW THAT YOU HAVE a new vision for your Next-Level Life and have given yourself permission to authentically claim all you want, it's time to deepen the inner commitment to your dream with Step Three: Declare Your Dream.

Move beyond the safe confines of your journal and bring your dream into the open by speaking out loud about what you aspire to achieve. To successfully optimize this step, it's important to be mindful about how and when you speak about your desire; if not, you could be waylaid by your own fears and doubts, or by the discomfort of others.

There are two areas of your communication that we will explore in-depth to fully Declare Your Dream:

> **Your inner dialogue** - the thoughts we silently communicate to ourselves.

> **Your outer dialogue** - how we express our ideas and thoughts to others.

The thoughts you think and the words you speak have a tremendous impact on the outcomes of your life. **The results you have today are the product of the thoughts, words, and actions you've generated until this point.** You create and experience from the exact level you are thinking and speaking. To crack the code and reach your Next-Level Life, you must be more conscious and intentional. It's critical that you are mindful of how you think and speak about your dreams and goals.

Inner Dialogue

Let's start by exploring all the facets of how inner dialogue works in your life and in the creation of your dreams.

Ask yourself:

Does my inner self-talk align with or against my dreams and goals?

Do I make excuses such as, "I don't have the time," "It costs too much," or similar reasons?

Do I feel like I am in a back-and-forth tug of war, in which my heart "wants what it wants," whereas my inner critic tells me, "Don't go for it; it's not going to work out"?

Our running verbal monologue is ongoing and nonstop. Until you bring awareness to what you are saying to yourself, your inner dialogue loops endlessly. Unfortunately, much of the time, your inner commentary has a negative bias. Even the most positive of us can slip into the habit of making judgments about others or offering unkind commentary and complaints to ourselves and others. This nonstop and unproductive stream of thoughts weighs us down, keeping us stuck and unable to move forward. What is going on here?

When you pay attention to how you talk to yourself, you can see where you are holding yourself back *and* you can course-correct it. Behavior change starts with awareness. Change your thoughts and change your language; you will be in a better place to identify and declare your dream. You can change the direction of your life. The reason why you can't seem to make progress even when you dare to dream big and try new behaviors that would support that dream is that we are caught in a jail of our own creation: the inner conflict, a byproduct of our inner critic, and our dreamer waging a power play. The inner critic often wins because it's been the predominant voice for most of your life and the dreamer is just a whisper.

Here's how inner conflict plays out …

Energetically, there is a part of us that wants "the thing," and the other part is talking ourselves out of it. The dreamer's voice will tell us these sorts of positives: "To go for it" and "This really is a good idea," while the inner critic will pay defense, saying, "This is not a good idea. We should abandon this asap!" This kind of inner back-and-forth dialogue, coupled with the seesaw of emotions that accompany our thoughts, creates a standstill to progress. It's literally like having one foot on the gas pedal while at the same time, the other foot is on the brake. For this reason, many people take so long to achieve certain goals and wonder, in retrospect: Why did it take me so long?

As we discussed regarding neuroplasticity in Step Two, the subconscious mind accepts everything it receives. Everything. All of us can be easily susceptible to our inner critic running wild if it is left unchecked. Your goal is to build belief and energy toward what you truly want rather than unwittingly sabotaging yourself with critical, diminishing, or sarcastic statements such as:

I don't know who I think I am fooling. This isn't going to happen, not in this lifetime.

I don't have the funds to pull this off. Who in the world would give me money for my ideas?

She never supports my ideas, so I'm not going to bring it up.

I always attract the wrong guy. Always have, and probably always will.

I'm doomed to be what my DNA dictates, overweight like my family members. Nothing I can do about that. I've tried.

If I join this program, or get another certification, then I will be able to launch my business.

I don't have the energy or courage to follow through.

I don't know enough.

I don't have anyone to help me.

I don't need anyone to help me.

I feel too much anxiety about doing this, so I better wait.

I'm too old, or I'm too young.

The reality is that if you have a big, audacious dream that you have not achieved yet, it is certain that you have some inner house cleaning to do for your version of toxic thinking. The quickest way to turn this around is by becoming an observer of your own thoughts. You can do this by paying attention to what the "voice" in your head is saying to you. It will become more evident when you speak out loud what you write about in your journal posts. You'll start to catch your conflicting patterns of language—the negative statements you tell yourself that are non-supportive to you and your goal. The inner critic has often taken the stage and has stolen the show. No wonder you cannot make traction toward your goals! You are talking yourself out of what you want daily.

The critical statements above are variations of tolerations, those things you are putting up with or allowing to exist energetically in your life in a negative way. The good news is that you can shift negative self-talk to positive self-talk. Once you become aware of a belief that is holding you back, you can challenge the belief and ask: Is it true? Chances are that the belief isn't 100 percent true, at least not all the time. Once you have burst the bubble of that belief, you can remodel it into an intention that serves your dream, instead of diminishing it. Your inner critic can become your inner cheerleader!

Ask yourself: Am I more devoted to my old story of problems and perceived shortcomings or to my new story of Next-Level Life? Reprogramming your mind is a function of overriding the current inner critic's operating system and installing empowering intentions.

All the limiting labels you have given yourself is a mirage that you accidentally believe to be true. Consciously or unconsciously, you will believe whatever you tell yourself, so you might as well choose to tell yourself what you want! Isn't this a great reminder? At this moment in time, you can release yourself from the past by declaring first to yourself, "This is what I want *now*."

Our intentions create the pathway to our Next-Level Life.

Did you know that quantum physicist William Tiller discovered that the mere act of observation will affect the outcome? Tiller discovered this it is possible to affect change in a sub-atomic particle by holding a clear intention to do so. In a famous experiment called the Double Slit Experiment, which involved observing energy patterns of both waves and particle forms, it was observed that when the experimenter intended to see particles, that is precisely what was observed. When they intended to see waves instead of particles, that was what researchers observed. These findings indicate that you have the capacity to influence your own reality by using conscious intention. You may not be able to change a large mass object (like a dog into a lion) but research shows that your conscious focus can influence your outcomes.

An effective way to consciously focus is to get into the habit of cleaning up any rogue negative thoughts and beliefs and upgrading them into new intentions. You can customize the perfect intentions (mantras) to match your desired results.

I like to choose a mantra that I am resonating with and write it on a sticky note and put it on my computer. Even when

I don't think I notice it, I am priming my subconscious mind, which does see it and absorbs it, by adding another layer of imprinting of this positive intention into my neural pathways.

Here are some of my favorite (universal for any goal) mantras:

Instead of: I am so challenged with ongoing health issues.
Every day, in every way, I am getting better and better.

Instead of: I don't have that kind of money to invest.
The universe supplies all that I need to achieve this goal.

Instead of: I don't have experience or luck with organizing big projects.
I am amply supported in all that I choose to do.

Here are a few more great universal mantras:

My timing is perfect.
Everything is always working out in my favor.
What I want wants me.
I am divinely guided.
Everything is for me.
I am a magnet for abundance, health, and prosperity.

I encourage you to make up your own!

Let's revisit Adrian's vision in the context of language repatterning. In a coaching session, Adrian clarified his vision and, with excitement, articulated his new story and declared his dream with me. Here's what Adrian declared: He was going to move to a new city, and establish a dynamic lifestyle that included the arts, a like-minded community, and a wide variety of entertainment options. His new home and furniture would soon reflect his love for a comfortable and modern style.

He envisioned the perfect new role at a progressive company and set his sights on significantly increasing his income and financial acumen. For the most part during this share, he was enthusiastic, however, his tone, inflection, and the words he spoke revealed some underlying hesitancy. As he shared his brand-new vision, he sprinkled in a couple of disclaimers, including: "I will probably need to slow this down. My family— especially my mom—will really be upset if I moved to another city, especially now when there is a new baby in the mix."

Another area of his vision that he was holding back on was around his finances. He said, "I should probably hold off on the job search for a while so I can save up more money first." We both caught it. In the couple of minutes it took to share his vision and these "under the radar" disclaimers, Adrian recognized that he was still not 100 percent on board with his own dreams. As we talked and sorted through it, he realized that he was blocking his own progress with old ideas of what was true or not. Like a newborn calf, his new vision had shaky legs and could barely stand at first. By declaring his vision out loud, he was able to address what was concerning him and tap into what his wishes were. Those wishes transformed into new intentions.

Here are some of the mantras that Adrian added to his inner dialogue:

> I trust myself completely.
>
> My dream will unfold in perfect timing.
>
> I am resourceful and fully supported.
>
> When I act on my own behalf, it has a positive ripple effect on others, especially my family.
>
> I am a magnet for money and perfect opportunities.

Once Adrian repatterned his language by adding these specific and meaningful intentions to his dream, his energy shifted.

Notice that, in order to move forward with your vision and create your future desirable experiences, you must check in with your inner dialogue. Sometimes our resistance is hiding right beneath the surface, and by stating our story out loud to ourselves and in our journal, these limiting beliefs can be caught and cleaned up. Tell a new story, and your mind will readily accept the mantras you give to it. Not only that, but our brain will also immediately be on alert for evidence of people, places, and opportunities that resonate with your new storyline. Be kind to yourself and speak positively to yourself, creating your own self-fulfilling prophecy. If you think you can, or you think you can't, you're probably right! Right here, right now, you can direct where you are going, and it starts with what you are believing and telling yourself daily. We have nothing to lose and everything to gain by attempting the miraculous in our lives.

Another way to declare our dreams to ourselves is with the use of positive statements about ourselves and the dream in the form of an "I am" statement. What is an I am statement? It is an affirmation of what you would like to be, have, or do should you achieve your dream, starting the affirmation with "I am …"

Here are some examples:

I am living and loving my summers in Tuscany.

I am a fluid and joyful dancer on the dance floor.

I am deeply peaceful.

I am financially free.

I am radiant with confidence, certainty, and optimism.

I am in the best physical shape of my life.

I am surrounded and blessed with loving friends and family.

I am well-connected.

I am spiritually guided and positive.

I am a clear communicator.

I am open to the goodness and the abundance of the universe.

I am effectively communicating my needs and desires.

I am blessed.

I am inspiring.

I am creative.

I am always connected to my higher power.

I am a successful owner of a thriving and highly profitable business that makes a positive difference to our customers.

I am intuitive.

I am powerful, I am loving, and I am loved.

I am rich beyond measure.

I am enjoying my high integrity, high-end clients who are deeply committed to their transformation and dreams.

I am capable of creating anything I choose.

I am a magnet for new and wonderful opportunities.

Outer Dialogue

Now that we have covered inner dialogue, let's get curious about how you talk with and to others about yourself and your dreams. I first want to ask you these core questions:

How do you talk about your dreams to other people?

Whom are you sharing your vision with?

Are you sharing your vision with or without discernment?

If you are a person who tells everyone everything and is not discriminating, you may get overwhelmed by the multitudes of opinions. Then there are folks who don't tell anyone and keep their dream too tight to the vest. They find safety in being protective but do a disservice because they are not getting accountability or support for their dream.

What is the balance of sharing our dream for our Next-Level Life? If you do decide to share, how do you know if someone is "safe" and can be trusted?

Let's look at some scenarios that would be positive to share:

Trusted Allies

As I was becoming more and more aligned with my Big Dream of moving cross country to San Diego, all the while, I had a unit of three strong allies. Each of these allies were coaches like me and the four of us were champions of one another. These three amigos had been with me during the time that I birthed my San Diego vision, and they showed up relentlessly with their support. Whenever I was visiting San Diego, the four of us would meet to do progress check-ins and celebrate each of our Next-Level Life dreams progress.

This occasion was no exception. We first had a lovely dinner at Cafe Gratitude (a vegan restaurant that names each entree as an affirmation such as "I am grateful" or "I am abundant"). What a perfect place for four coaches to spend their evening!

At the dinner, I announced my wish to lead a three-day workshop in San Diego. This was a huge leap for me. At that time, I had only done seminars in Ohio. Planning a big event like this from across the country was expensive and complicated. I shared my vision with my trusted allies. They were 100 percent supportive. Their complete faith and belief in me helped to boost my confidence and own my vision. It was an overwhelming thought to have a seminar out of state. Declaring the event made it real, but I was concerned about the financial risk and the fear that no one would sign up for the event. My friends counterbalanced my fears with their extreme belief in me.

The experience of having my trusted trio who completely believed in me gave me wings to go for it and fly. To top off this moment of personal victory, the Universe decided we must now go celebrate this decision. We paid our dinner check and walked over to the Little Italy district in San Diego to Extraordinary Desserts, a cafe that serves, yep, you guessed, *only* extraordinary desserts. What a high-vibe evening. We each ordered a slice of luscious cake, and, between bites, we toasted my newly declared dream.

The event was on.

While this decision wasn't directly related to my moving to San Diego, it was an action step that could solidify my presence in San Diego. I was stepping more and more into the energy of "Yes to San Diego." Being selective about to whom and when I shared this vision made all the difference.

Postscript: The San Diego event was extraordinary (just like the cake) and was so successful that I repeated the event the following year!

Family, Friends & Coworkers

So, what is the best course of action when it comes to sharing our dreams with family, friends, and colleagues? Sharing with family and well-meaning friends can be a double-edged sword.

After all, they are our closest loved ones. Should you tell them everything about your life, especially this exciting new quest that you have recently launched? If you know your Aunt Susan is a hard-core pessimist and downer, she's definitely not the person to confide your newly hatched dream to.

Without a doubt, your loved ones have opinions and ideas about you and may hold a "loving" agenda for you. They can't help it! They have the best possible intentions for you and your welfare, but it's framed through a lens of *their* ideas about who you are, wanting to protect you, keep you safe, or not wanting aspects of your relationship to change.

It is entirely possible that your dream may have repercussions that will impact your relationships, so it makes sense that your loved ones might push back a bit (or a lot) and attempt to talk you out of your dream. Sadly, there are dream killers out there.

If your Next-Level Life could talk to you, it would ask you to be a good steward of your vision.

Sharing with friends can be similar. With friends there might be an added dimension of unconscious jealousy or competition that is masked by "concern for you." Your friend challenges your thinking by saying, "Nicole, you couldn't possibly do that! Don't take that risk; your family and friends will not approve."

Or you might get judgment served up to you in a passive-aggressive style, which sounds like, "Sure, go ahead and leave your good friends behind while you go off and live your new life in Italy. I hope you'll remember me after you go. Are you sure you really want to do this?" Comments like these can instantly take the wind out of your sails and deflate your motivation and cast the seeds of self-doubt.

Worst-case scenario, when you take on your friends' and family members' projected fears and judgments as truth, you could forget your own truth. How others react and project onto you can affect you by giving you the back door to slip out of and abandon your dream.

In 2015, Dr. Gail Matthews, a Dominican University psychology professor, conducted a study on goal-setting. The research findings showed that documenting one's goal raises the rate of success, but the factor that boosted success rates (up to 76 percent) was adding two key behaviors: verbally sharing the goal and providing weekly progress updates with a friend or coach. These two actions created accountability and solidified the results. So, we can see that declaring our dream is an effective strategy!

Your vision is something precious and should be treated with tender loving care as it grows and gets stronger in your belief and execution of it. Share your vision with someone who cannot only handle it as a potential reality but is actively cheering you on.

Here is how my client Rae utilized declaring her dream.

Rae's Next-Level Life dream was to leave the corporate world and launch her own consulting/coaching business. Her dream was fresh and new, and it would require some time before it could come to pass, but she believed in it and got busy building it. In the meantime, she continued to fulfill her role as an employee at the current company. She was doing well with both. Her excitement about her next-level career goals fueled her energy at work, too. In fact, she was so inspired by her dream that it spilled over into her day-to-day work. She woke up every morning with renewed meaning to her life and a sense of purpose in her current position.

Rae gave her best to her team and the company. Her inner self-talk was positive and generative. She wanted to share her exciting plans with others but decided to think it through first. Who could she confide in? She had several work friends with whom she could confide her exciting vision for her Next -Level Life, but she decided to share her vision with only one person there. She knew that her secret dream was not only safe, but her friend would cheer her on *and* hold her feet to the fire. Rae did the inner and outer work to manifest her dreams. A key piece of this success, according to Rae, was her weekly check-in with her supportive friend. Within one year, her dreams came to fruition.

Personal Development Events

Stating your dream out loud at an event catered to building up your personal esteem and direction is another way to gain momentum and support. If you recall, one of the activities in my Dream Big event mentioned in the prior chapter was having participants design their own vision boards. Once they were created, in a show-and-tell style, each table proudly presented their creations to one another. As I created an environment that was positive and safe, participants felt okay sharing with people they had not known for long. Taking turns, each person explained the significance of their imagery and told the story of their dream.

It was riveting to observe that, as each person declared their dream, the entire table responded with enthusiasm, curiosity, and genuine interest. The camaraderie I witnessed with this group was inspiring. After hearing one another share their dreams, attendees chimed in with resources, support, contacts, and ideas, and they exchanged cell numbers. This group not only had their Next-Level Life depicted on their vision board, but they also left the event with a higher level of belief and excitement, *and* many had new contacts and resources that would help them execute their Next-Level Life goals.

In the story of the Dream Big workshop, the attendees had a common goal in that they were there to bring their dreams alive. One of the women, Donna, shared with me later how impactful it was for her to leave this event having made some of her strongest allies with her table partners, who were strangers to her before the workshop. This sentiment was echoed by each of the women. They now had a community and promised to be there for each other as they each moved forward with their plans.

Donna shared she had decided to keep her vision private except for the people she bonded with at the Dream Big event. She went on to explain that she truly felt their support, and there was no competition or agenda interfering with her decisions. This lit a fire within to start taking action on her vision. Donna received an infusion of courage and left the event ready to play full-out thanks to declaring her dream. (This is why mastermind coaching groups can be so valuable for growth-minded people with Next-Level dreams.)

Within this step, Declare Your Dream, you've learned important distinctions when it comes to how you speak of your Next-Level Life vision. The first place to start as you frame your dream is to pay attention to how you talk to yourself. Your inner dialogue is an excellent litmus test of your alignment with your dream. If your beliefs are faulty and are not supportive to your vision, the framework for your dream can come apart. Tending to your thoughts is a worthwhile pursuit.

You've learned in this chapter the razor's edge of our beliefs. Our self-talk is either a contribution to our ascension or a boulder in the way of our desired path. The good news is that your beliefs are malleable. Once you have exposed a faulty belief, you can deliberately reshape it into its higher expression of an empowering statement. Quality thoughts are equal to quality results.

Your outer dialogue is also a key component to fashioning your Next-Level Life. To boost your success, choose a supportive ally, someone you trust implicitly who will be rooting you on as you continue to progress higher and higher with your Big Dream. This outward declaration of your dream is an essential component to creating momentum and accountability.

Timing

Timing is another essential factor. In the beginning phase of dream building, the idea is so new and often so daunting that we don't have an abundance of confidence … yet. So, being careful about whom you share your dream with is important. Be judicious and err on the side of caution. You don't want to get talked out of something you haven't even been given a chance with. With time, and by practicing visualization and incorporating visual imagery into your environment, you will strengthen your conviction and belief in yourself and the ability to manifest this dream of yours. As you feel more confident, more in flow and secure with your vision, you may feel more apt to share it with others.

Again, be mindful of whom you share with and what your motivation is to share it with them. Only share if you feel it will add to your momentum. Don't do it if you have reservations about it. If you have reservations, it's not time to share it yet with that person. Trust your instincts.

There is a power behind sharing our dreams and goals with supportive others. The dreams/goals become even more real. When you hear yourself speak out loud to someone (such as a trusted friend, or better yet, your coach) who is listening deeply and is holding space for you as you share your vision, you grow from your "true" confession. This kind of conversation empowers you to respect your dream and treat it as something that is real and something that can be achieved.

The dream is a tangible reality that can be explored and manifested. Declaring our dream is the catalyst for us. You go from nervously sharing to boldly claiming your desires, and this sets the stage for taking the actions to make this dream a reality.

Your Turn

Who is a safe and supportive ally to share your dream with?

_____

_____

_____

Declaring your dream is thrilling and scary at the same time. It takes courage to go big, to really pursue the next level in your life. If you feel imposter syndrome creeping into your psyche, it's a great sign that you are on the right path! This may seem counterintuitive, but it is a sure sign that you are going beyond the status quo in your life. Give yourself a big high-five! This is worthy of your acknowledgement. It takes courage to step into your dreams.

Your dream deserves to come true.

and

This is the time to have courage.

What does courage have to do with a dream? Turns out, quite a lot. The origin of the English word courage is the French word _coeur,_ which means "from the heart." Next-level dreams and goals come from the heart. These are intentions that are deep, exciting, and can seem impossible. The risk to share with another becomes a gift you receive. When you speak your heart's desires with a trusted ally, you'll discover that it feels good to be seen, heard, and validated. It sparks the flame of courage deep within you that, yes, I **can** do this. This inner courage is alive within you and is like the wind beneath your wings as you take flight with manifesting your Next-Level Life.

Sharing it out loud helps solidify the vision you have penned into your journal. It's released into the "wild." It's out in the open as a full-fledged goal with intention infused in it *and* you've got yourself and a trusted person in your corner, smiling and encouraging you to keep going!

Let's do a pulse check … By wading through some of your challenges and discontent, you come out of Step One victorious with the Wish List. With your list, you've captured your preferences and desires and then shaped them into your vision in Step Two by utilizing neuroscience best practices, mental visioning, and creating a visual representation of your dream using a vision board. In Declare Your Dream, we look at how to articulate your new story from that visioning work with language that fortifies your vision and subsequent actions toward your Next-Level Life. We took a deep dive into how and when to speak our dreams into existence.

I acknowledge you for your efforts so far! Are you ready to go farther with your dreams? In the upcoming chapter, Step Four: Design Your Dreams, your Next-Level Life will grow in its strength and trajectory.

Like Adrian, when you become stronger and more aligned with your vision, you will be able to move into Step Four: Be the Architect of Your Dream and map out your blueprint with actionable steps and timelines. Let's keep the momentum going!

CHAPTER 7

Step Four: Be the Architect of Your Dream

"Every action you take is a vote for the person you wish to become."

James Clear

NOW WE GET YOUR Big Dream into action in Step Four: Be the Architect of Your Dream. In the last chapter, Declare Your Dream, I had you shouting your dream from the mountaintop. Okay, maybe you weren't that excited yet, but I have led you to paint a picture of your vision and declare this dream to not only yourself but also to a trusted ally or two. In Step Three, you also committed to be more conscious of building your dream using positive inner dialogue. Now the time has come in this step to design your own blueprint, which will serve to take your big lofty dream and turn it into a specific, measurable, and attainable plan.

Sounds unglamorous, but our goal is to make what seemed so big just a short time ago into a new fact of life for you. One of the biggest dilemmas you face when you claim your dream is the enormity of it! You might ask yourself, *How on earth do I add my Big Dream to my already-overflowing daily schedule?* Sometimes our dream can feel so big and out of the realm of what is possible that we short-circuit it and give it up before we allow our dream the opportunity to develop. I don't want that for you!

To realize your Big Dream, you must give it space in your life. By embracing our dreams and holding them close to our heart the way forward becomes more visible and doable.

By establishing a plan, you will complete three steps ending up with an actual blueprint that serves as your guide to getting from here to there. As the architect of your dream, that blueprint is vital before you can begin constructing your high-rise dream. Your Next-Level Goals and action steps translate into the building materials of your amazing new creation. All of these amazing things are impossible to pull off unless you've got a plan to guide the way.

Note that just thinking of your dream and designing it with a vision can't manifest it. You need to take actionable steps. The secret to success with action steps is the organization of a blueprint. We take the huge, overarching goal of your Next-Level Life and break it down into the Next-Level Goals and sub-goals and, from there, define your action steps and timelines. It's a practical process, and by completing this step, your confidence will be increased. You will have a roadmap, not just an idea of your dream's vision dancing solo in your head.

The three working parts of designing tour dream blueprint are:

1. **Telescope Into Your Future -** This part has us going three years into the future with our next-level dream to capture additional information and establish timelines for our dream. By telescoping out, we can see more clearly the pathway to our dreams (it's also a great boost to our motivation). Projecting our ideal vision into the near future provides us with important pieces of our dream, including specific goals (which are your Next-Level Goals).
2. **Plan It Out -** Once you have telescoped into your future, document your Next-Level Goals. From here, you take each next-level goal and list the subgoals and the action steps associated to reach your main goals.
3. **Your Dream Blueprint -** Your Dream Blueprint is your living document and serves as your guide to your Next-Level Life. Once you've mapped it out, you will have completed and designed our own customized dream blueprint.

These three parts—telescoping, planning it out, and the creation of your dream blueprint—gives you a clear and tangible path forward.

Let's begin designing!

The Telescoping Exercise

The purpose of this exercise is to expand your sense of what is possible for you. Many of us are conditioned to think primarily in a logical and linear way. You become so tied to what "makes sense" that you bypass your fertile creative imagination or dismiss a new idea. This limited approach to dreaming about your Next-Level life will keep you playing small.

My invitation to you is to soften the rules around what you think you are capable of manifesting. In the book *Originals: How Non-Conformists Move the World* author Adam Grant states, "Originals are non-conformists, and they not only have new ideas, but they are willing to champion those ideas with action." So, let's prime you for your Next-Level Life by first connecting to the energy you want to create for your Next-Level Life. Tap into the emotions of the goals you aspire to. If your Next-Level Life is to live in Paris, what will it feel like to be living there as the Parisians do?

Take a moment to tap into the emotions you want to feel in your Next-Level Life.

Good, now let's dive into your imagination and cultivate the delicious dream you wish to make your reality.

Find a quiet place where you feel at ease and with no distractions. As you sink into your comfortable space, consciously let go of any worries, cares, and concerns. For now, allow yourself to luxuriate in a nice and easy relaxed state. If you find that your mind is busy with lots of thoughts, know this is normal. Simply regroup and come back to your own state of relaxation.

Gently close your eyes. Observe your breathing. Allow your breath to cycle in and out, flowing in a natural pace.

In the book *Breath* by James Nestor, the author shares that just a few rounds of intentional and relaxed breathing change our body chemistry, reduce stress, increase creativity, and balance masculine and feminine energy. And who doesn't want or need that?

Now that you are in this deep state of relaxation and receptivity, we are ready to take a trip into the future … With your eyes closed, imagine that you have magically been transported into the future three years from now. Your Big Dream has come true, every bit of it, and it is even more amazing than you thought possible.

Be sure to stay in the present moment of your dream. Be in it right now. Notice all the details, from what you are wearing to whom you are with to the location you are in. Pay attention to it all. See it but also feel it. Allow yourself to have a full-body experience.

Now that you are zoomed into your Next-Level Life with the vision that you created of your dream back in Step Two, you can start to ask experiential questions. What is it like for you to be you living your Next-Level Life? How does this dream appear in your actual life? The key to this exercise is to tap into your emotions of the feeling as you envision living this new life.

Write down your experience, full of excitement that this is what you are living as if it is happening RIGHT NOW.

I have also given sample answers I have seen through coaching thousands of Big Dream seekers through this process. *(You can write in the space provided in the book, but as I know you will have more than one dream. I suggest you use this as a template for dreams as you have them..*

Dream It, Design It, Live It

Where are you? *(Insert location of your Big Dream.)*

_____

What are you doing, experiencing, and enjoying?
(This could be a new profession, state of mind, change of schedule, more financial freedom, and/or a fulfilling relationship.)

_____

Who have you become in the past three years to achieve this dream?
(Someone who believes in themselves and also trusts beyond my "to-do list" to a higher order. I am more confident. I am living with more integrity and authenticity.)

What obstacles did you overcome to get to this place?
(Doubt, financial fear, judgment from others, low self-worth, and unforeseen roadblocks.)

_____

What did you learn about yourself?
(Resiliency and trust. Progress without perfection. Stop comparing myself to others).

_____

_____

What does it mean to you to have this Big Dream realized?
(That I get to live the way I want, and this is so important to me. It's a dream come true. I have learned so much about myself. My life is better in so many ways because I prioritized myself and honored my dream.)

_____

How are you demonstrating your most important values in life?
(I stayed true to myself and that is a match to my value of integrity. I also am living my values of creativity, adventure, and community.)

_____

_____

_____

Write down any insights you have on new goals or timelines.
(I feel more empowered to take actions on my goals.)

_____

_____

_____

Beautiful job! Now that you have expanded your vision of your dream in an experiential way, what else are you aware of that you didn't realize until now?

In order to be the confident person three years from now, you have seen you may need a new skill, or to repair a relationship, or change where or how you live. What are you proud of that you have overcome to get here? What's new about who you are? Perhaps you have become more confident, more creative, and freer. More YOU!

We often make decisions that might not come to fruition for months or years. We also have relationships we need to be honest or courageous about, where there are people who need to be invested in our dream because they are impacted. Understanding the pieces that need to line up in your future puts a realistic aspect on your timeline.

The reason that I recommend a three-year-timespan for projecting into your future is because it a reasonable and manageable chunk of time. Five years is hard to hold in our minds, but if we only look ahead one year, it is not the whole picture if we have a Big Dream.

The telescoping exercise opens more nuances and perspectives. You can recognize situations where you may not be factoring in some roadblocks or uncomfortable scenarios that need to be addressed. You will have the whole picture of your beautiful dream, and this exercise will expand your vision into a multidimensional experience.

For example, if your secret dream is to become a real estate superstar in Hawaii, then there will be obvious logistics that you will need to track that could take some time to produce results. There may be specific obstacles or growth-related items that you would need to experience in order to get from point

A to point B. Doing this telescoping exercise will help you bring both the tangible steps and your personal growth-related awareness into focus.

Congratulations! By allowing yourself to freely imagine your personal truth as you telescope into your future, you added depth and texture to your dream and have also captured additional goals and a better perspective on your timeframes. In addition, because of the multidimensional aspect of this meditation, you've added another layer of neural pathways and primed another level of your belief in your own dream. Now, let's get granular and complete the second part of designing your dream, *Plan It Out.*

The secret to realizing Big Dreams is that we must take that big audacious dream and break it down into smaller, bite-sized pieces.

Plan It Out

Now you have the vision of your Next-Level Life fresh in your mind's eye, let's take your telescoped vision and plan it out. It is important to take your desired vision and map it out on paper so that you have a working plan. When you convert your dream into a well-thought-out plan, it allows both sides of your brain (the creative and the linear) to work together on behalf of the dream and enables you to have a blueprint that guides your actions.

The first priority is to deconstruct your dream by breaking it down into your main Next-Level Goals and associated subgoals. Once you have those defined, you can logically determine the sequence of small action steps needed to accomplish the goals. The reason this is vital to do first is based on years of research on best practices for achieving success.

In a study completed in 1980, Edwin A. Locke, an American psychologist, and a pioneer in goal-setting theory, identified a positive correlation between goal setting and success. Locke, who reviewed a decade of research from 1969 to 1980, found that the simple act of writing down and tracking goals led to higher performance 90 percent of the time. Yes, you read that correctly—90 percent of the time!

In 1990, Locke partnered with Gary Latham, PhD., a professor of Organizational Effectiveness at the Rotman School of Management at the University of Toronto, and in their study, they identified that, once again, goal setting is a powerful technique that leads to better performance.

It turns out that when we document our goals, and they are aspirational, we are motivated to higher levels of effort as compared to those who don't write down their goals and plans. Let this sink in! You can join the most successful people on the planet who know that goal setting and project planning are key to the personal and professional results you want.

To start the Plan It Out process, begin with the Big Dream of Your Next-Level Life. For example, I named my dream blueprint "The San Diego Dream." Feel free to name your dream in a way that speaks to you. One of my client's called her dream blueprint "My Parisian Life." Another called hers "White Picket Fence" (her dream was to find her soulmate, get married, and start a family).

What is the name of your dream?

Write it here:

_____

Name Your Main Goals (Next-Level Goals)

For each one, name, define, and map out action steps and time-lines. Like the specific measurements and drawings needed for a good blueprint, these Next-Level Goals are the information you need to build your ultimate creation—your Next-Level Life.

Here's an example of how to map out Next-Level Goals.

My client Portia came to coaching with the goal to pursue her next-level dream. She was successful and ambitious but was stuck with how to manifest her Next-Level Life. Portia's dream was to create a whole new lifestyle for herself and her family. As the owner of her own growing real estate office in San Francisco, she was enjoying the fruits of her labor. In the past four years, her business doubled in revenue each year. The system she set up was working like a charm. She had a loyal and productive team.

However, her dream was to replicate her success with a second office in Maui. Why Maui? She had loved the island vibe of Hawaii and the international, high-end luxury real estate. It was both a thrill and challenge for her.

Portia's dream included providing her children a lifestyle that was more relaxed and easygoing than the highly competitive, driven vibe that San Francisco offered. She also wanted to support her daughter's desire to surf competitively and to grow up in paradise. Her vision was that she and her children would live in Hawaii during the school year, and the children would return to California to spend summers with their father (her ex-husband).

Portia had a big "aha" moment when she completed the telescoping exercise. She realized that for her dream to come true, she would have to improve her contentious relationship with her ex-husband so they could decide together what was best for their children. This realization created a next-level goal that she had not planned for (that of improving her relationship with her ex-husband), but without it, her dream would be stalled without her ex-husband's buy-in to her vision.

Here is an example of Portia's Next-Level Life dream:

Mission Aloha

Next-Level Goal 1- Set up a thriving luxury real estate office in Maui, Hawaii.

Next-Level Goal 2 - Make peace with my children's father.

Next-Level Goal 3 - Find our dream home, community, and school.

Portia created specific goals with a name, clear definition, and action plan with timelines. Like the details of a blueprint, these Next-Level Goals are the makeup of Portia's ultimate creation—her Next-Level Life.

Next, Portia looked at each Next-Level Goal and asked one by one: What are the subgoals related to each of these goals? Here is how she did that:

> Next-Level Goal - Set up a thriving luxury real estate office in Maui, Hawaii
>
> Subgoal 1 - Do online market research on Maui real estate transactions and forecasts.
>
> Subgoal 2 - Research competitive agents/offices in the area.
>
> Subgoal 3 - Research what options exist for my real estate office space.
>
> Subgoal 4 - Define the logistics/requirements to set up a business in Hawaii.

As you can see, her next-level goal to open a Maui real estate office required her to identify what she needed to accomplish for this main goal to be realized. At first, this exercise seems complicated, but I assure you that it's intuitive, and using the template will help you to fill in the main goals and subgoals quickly.

Once you have determined your subgoals, then you can take each of these and define your action steps in a logical sequence using the question: What will I need to do first? What is next? Continue in this way until you have fleshed out specific actions you will need to take.

In the above example, Portia's Subgoal 1 was to do online market research on Maui real estate transactions and forecasts. For Portia to meet this goal, she had to ask herself: What is the first step I need to take and when will I take the action? To accomplish this subgoal, Portia determined her first action step was to spend the next two weekends researching and taking notes on both transactions and forecasts. Her second step, completing the research piece, was to schedule a meeting with her mentor to review the results and determine next steps from this meeting.

Here's a snapshot of how this looked on Portia's blueprint:

Next-Level Goal 1 - Set up a thriving luxury real estate office in Maui, Hawaii.

Subgoal 1 - Do online market research on Maui real estate transactions and forecasts.

Action Steps/Date:

1. Spend the next two weekends researching and taking notes on both transactions and forecasts.

2. Meet with mentor to review findings.

3. Create a report to reference for future meetings with banks, government officials, etc.

This process of mapping out goals is surprisingly simple yet comprehensive. The template you will use is designed so you can quickly map out your own blueprint. By breaking down the parts of the goal into subgoals and the actions we need to take with deadlines, we've quickly designed our own "project plan." So, in the example of Portia and her Next-Level Goals, she continued to map out the sequence of each subgoal and list the action steps that were associated with the execution of that subgoal.

As a result of doing the telescoping exercise, Portia also gained awareness of a personal goal—to make peace with her ex-husband, the father of her children. This new goal is integral to success in her Next-Level Life. When Portia did the visioning exercise of her dream life, this piece of unfinished business with her ex-husband hadn't occurred to her. Now, she could factor this important goal into her plan, as they are inter-related. The blueprint also gives you a reality check.

Another aspect that was fine-tuned in the telescoping exercise was a better calculation of her timeline. As she mapped out all her Next-Level Goals and subgoals, she was able to establish realistic benchmarks.

The beauty of your blueprint is that it is not rigid; it is an ever-evolving plan through which you track your progress and stay accountable to yourself.

As you courageously commit to your blueprint and begin to tackle the sub-goals related to your desired outcome, you gain traction with your goals. As you begin to feel positive movement forward, you will also feel a rise in inner motivation and confidence. Albert Bandura, PhD, calls this effect self-efficacy. Self-efficacy, as it relates to goals, translates as an internal acknowledgment that we are taking control and making strides forward, and this adds to our persistence to keep going.

Another interesting piece of research that underscores the validity of creating your blueprint and mapping out goals and corresponding actions is the work of Stanford University professor and psychologist Dr. BJ Fogg. Professor Fogg coined the term "tiny habits" and has a book called *Tiny Habits: The Small Changes That Change Everything*. Fogg states that to do big things, get into the habit of doing small things to achieve the results you aim for.

Our brain is designed to be energy efficient. When you take the time to establish a plan with the action steps laid out before you, your mind can relax because it no longer must overthink how to accomplish this huge goal. Tiny actions done consistently will take you to the outcomes you desire. Step by step, you get closer to your desired finish line.

Your Dream Blueprint

Once you mapped out your Next-Level Goals, you have your own customized plan of action, your Dream Blueprint. Consider your Dream Blueprint as your new best friend, as it will serve you well as your trusty one-page Next-Level Life planning tool.

With your Blueprint in hand, the invisible is now visible, and you literally can start making headway in building out your dream by taking necessary actions based on your top priorities. You now have clarity and precision because each of your actionable items has been assigned a due date. You know where you are heading and have the pathway to get there.

Your Dream Blueprint will serve as your guide as you move toward your Next-Level Life. The secret to realizing Big Dreams is to take the audacious dream and break it down into smaller, bite-sized pieces, which you have done!

Now that you have established your Dream Blueprint, you get to choose which next-level goal to tackle first. Once you've identified that, begin to work through the natural sequence of subgoals and action steps that you've mapped out. Depending on the complexity of your goals, actions, and timeframes, you will likely be working on a few different items in the weeks and months ahead.

What is so helpful about having your Blueprint is that you can use it to monitor your progress, checking off the items that you've handled. You'll also be able to make modifications to your plan, perhaps adding an action item or deleting one.

The Dream Blueprint is replicated for each of your Next-Level Goals. Doing this helps keep things compact and clear as you work on one of the main goals that you have. Personally, I like to have my main Blueprint and, from that, create a separate one for some of my more complex Next-Level Goals. Doing this allows you to zero in on your "mini" project planning for one of your Next-Level Goals. Again, it may seem like this is a lot to decipher and to map out, but I promise it isn't difficult. Once you sit down with your vision, and identify your main goals, the rest flows onto paper.

Prioritization is your golden key for integrating your new blueprint into your day-to-day life. Truth is, this is a challenging task because of the multiple competing demands each of us has in our lives. How do we get it all accomplished? That is the question we will answer next!

How to Prioritize Your Dream

Your newly hatched Next-Level Goals deserve to be incorporated into your weekly planning now, even if the timeline is well into the future. It is vital that you take action even if they are micro-actions in pursuit of a visible next step. Energetically and neurochemically, you are sending a message to yourself and the Universe that you are serious about your Next-Level Life, that it's not just a wishful daydream.

You may be wondering how to prioritize. Each of us has a broad variety of goals we are working toward on a daily and weekly basis. It's a good practice to determine what your top priorities are by reviewing your goals at regular intervals. If your Next-Level Life had a voice, it would be asking you to honor it by taking action on those goals that meet your criteria of the highest priority. Without a strategy in place to lean into and animate your blueprint for our Next-Level Life, you might decide to delay your dream because you can't find a way to fit it into your already tightly packed calendar because there simply isn't space. This pattern continues day to day, week to week, and year to year, with our Big Dream collecting dust on a back shelf in our mind. This does not have to be the case for you!

Here's an approach that leads to faster and more spectacular results. It's called …

Big Dreams First

It's time for a mindset shift and to treat your Big Dream as royalty. Show your Next-Level Life respect by honoring and prioritizing your Blueprint and integrating the actions you need to take it into its rightful place in your calendar. Instead of relegating your dreams to a remote parking lot, put them into the "container" of your calendar first … then add the small/medium action items and pour in the tiny action items.

Personal development author Steven Covey uses the analogy of filling a container with a mix of sand, and small, medium, and big rocks to demonstrate how to manage our time. His analogy shows how to include our top-tier priorities daily. The way most people would fill the container is to fill it first with sand, then the small and medium rocks, and lastly attempt to squeeze in the big rocks. Filling the container in this way will not allow you to include all the items. However, if we reverse-engineer it and put the big rocks in first, then add the small and medium ones, and finally pour in the sand, the sand will fill the nooks and crannies created by the rocks. The point being that all the various rocks and stones and sand will fit into the container!

Instead of filling it with all our various-sized actions that may or may not be a top priority, let's put the Big Dreams first, and then layer everything else in. What you will discover is that, if you deliberately fill your calendar this way, you will discover that you can do more than you thought possible. Slowing down and taking the time to integrate the goals and actionable items of your blueprint into your current calendar will paradoxically help you to speed up your results.

By adopting this approach and depending on how big and complex and distant your dream timeline is, the fact is you will get there sooner if you start today. Even the smallest action is progress toward your desired outcome. Don't discount your progress!

Over time, the tiny action steps build on themselves and create significant momentum. Start by writing one paragraph. Start by making the first phone call. Start by doing research. Start by clearing debt. Just start! Be sure to give yourself credit for going toward your dream, check that off the list, and keep going!

Big Dreams are often complex, with a lot of details to attend to. It can be easy to fall into the trap of feeling overwhelmed (which is, of course, understandable but not ultimately necessary). As you stare down your dream and feel a wave of both fear and thrill at your beautiful dream, know that your Dream Blueprint is more than a plan. It's a guide that will help you find your way in new territory. Even if there are seemingly impossible obstacles to overcome when you look ahead at the dream you want to chase, know that, with a plan and determination, you can achieve mighty things. What gets measured gets done.

Setting Up Your Accountability Structures

Just like you declared your dream to get the ball rolling, now you need the next level of accountability. While your blueprint will also serve you to stay true to your goals, if left to our own devices, you may make excuses and delay acting. A self-delegated hall pass is a dangerous luxury to give into, especially when you delay taking actions that are tough to do.

If you really want to move to Hawaii and establish your real estate business there, yet you keep putting off booking a trip there or fail to sign up for getting your real estate license in Hawaii because you are feeling overwhelmed, you'll soon find that time has flown by, and you are not one inch closer to your dream.

A best-practice strategy is to have a designated person, such as a coach, mentor, or mastermind partner, hold your feet to the fire, especially during rough patches (when unforeseen obstacles crop up or your confidence takes a nosedive). It's smart to declare your plans to a trusted ally or two and create an accountability team.

Your Blueprint (beautiful and as detailed as it is) could evaporate into thin air if the only person you are staying accountable to is yourself.

You know how that feels when you are out of personal integrity. It feels terrible and gets worse the longer you delay acting toward something you truly want. It is common to use delay tactics when you are your sole accountability partner. You bargain and convince yourself that it isn't a good time (e.g., it isn't a great time to adopt a baby, invest in cryptocurrency, move to Hawaii, or fill in the blank).

The truth is there never is a perfect time. There is always something that you could justify as a reason that now isn't optimal. If you made all your decisions based on this story that now isn't a good time, you probably would not accomplish much of significance, especially when it comes to fulfilling your biggest dreams.

The bottom line is without setting up the infrastructure of your dream (by designing it, mapping out the action steps, and setting accountability) your dream may not get the chance to be born. I highly suggest finding those people you trust, such as a friend or a business associate, who has your back and wants you to succeed.

In picking your accountability team, it is helpful to consider the big picture and broaden the support you need by engaging a few accountability partners. Select different people for each aspect of the dream. For example, if you are getting stuck with the technology involved in the dream, you have the best person to help you out right away. If you are lacking confidence, who is the sunshine person who always sees the best in you and reflects that?

In addition to your accountability team, consider what other structures you could put in place to solidify sticking to your plan. These could range from inspirational sticky note messages to yourself to setting reminders on your phone. Another way to boost accountability is by getting into the habit of including the action items that relate to your dream goals directly into your weekly calendar. While your calendar can be all about honoring other people, you may need to get into the habit of carving out time for your truest priorities. The bottom line is that accountability is essential and worth taking time to define what exactly you need in order to stay with your plan and be successful. Some of us need more accountability than others, especially if the dream is big and requires us to make significant changes.

Who is on your accountability team?

_____

_____

What structures will you put in place?

_____

_____

_____

As I mentioned in Declare Your Dream, it's important to be judicious with whom you share your fragile, forming dream. What happens if the dream you envision is burning brightly in your heart and the people you share it with may not be on board for your big plan? Business or life partners may not see or feel how you do and have not bought into what you are trying to accomplish. There is no one-size-fits-all answer to how to manage this.

Anytime you dream big, the dream serves as a disruptor to the status quo. While this can rock the boat, and it's inevitable that there will be changes, it is a normal part of growth. This can be difficult terrain to be in, but it can be navigated. When your partner sees your ongoing commitment to your dream, they may warm up to the idea. Sometimes it just takes time.

I had the dream to be in a healthy and happy marriage and the dream to move across the country. One could have been in question. For me, it worked out because when our dream is true for us, while disruptive and people may not initially buy in, in the long run, what is true for us will have positive outcomes and ripples. I see this all the time for others, and having this knowledge can help you steer a fragile dream forward despite choppy waters for a period.

Now that you have followed steps one through four and have your Dream Blueprint, you are so much closer to a Next-Level Life than you know! Time for a mini-dance break to celebrate how much you have already put into motion for yourself! You have literally gone from ground zero, by sifting through where you are and where you want to be, getting honest about what is in your heart, and creating your new vision. You've done the work of upgrading your inner dialogue (calming that critical inner voice when it speaks up), and enlisting an ally or two to encourage you as you take actions step by step toward your beautiful Next-Level Life dream.

It's time to proceed to Part Three: Live It! We'll start with Dream Catalysts. In this next chapter, you will discover four unique practices to elevate your efforts and your mindset as you manifest more and more of your Big Dream. Let's dive in …

PART III

Live It: Achieve Your Dream Life

CHAPTER 8

Dream Catalysts

"What you seek is seeking you."

Rumi

MY **FAVORITE WAY TO** lead you to ignite your dream are the exercises that make up the Dream Catalysts. These four evidence-based methods are used to spark your own version of high-flame success.

Imagine you need to get a bonfire going. You want strong and robust flames to keep you warm or cook a meal. To do this, you'll need to have your materials at hand and strategically use them together (e.g., kindling, dry grass, paper, matches) to ignite sparks that come together to generate a full-fledged fire. That is exactly what this set of Dream Catalysts will do for you—stoke your goals with the energy they need to ensure the outcome of your biggest dream.

The four Dream Catalyst Exercises are:

> Exercise 1 – Morning Success Ritual
>
> Exercise 2 - Find Your Mirrors

Exercise 3- Stair-Stepping

Exercise 4 - Create Your Luck

Dream Catalyst Exercise 1: Morning Success Ritual

The secret to manifesting a Next-Level Life is to begin each day with clarity, focus, and intention. The way to do this is with a consistent morning success routine designed to allow you to be in charge of your day.

For a lot of us, our morning routine is "get up, get ready, and go!" The morning alarm sets us into frenzied motion, hurry to shower, grab a quick breakfast, and then hop into our car or onto our computers to get the workday started. If this sounds like you, you are in the majority.

The result of heading straight into your day without intention and clarity has a hidden cost. It's true that this "seize the day" mindset pushes you straight into action but it doesn't empower you to design your day with your priorities firmly in place. Without an intentional start to your day, **the day will own you if you don't own it first.**

The best place to start is by establishing a Morning Success Ritual. This exercise is a powerful process to spark peak performance and increase your peace and confidence daily.

You can establish simple logistics for you Morning Success Ritual. First, determine your optimal environment. You need to allow for quiet and uninterrupted time for just you. Choose a quiet space that allows you to reflect without distractions, such as your office, spare room, or porch. All you will need is your journal, your calendar, and your favorite morning beverage.

It's important to set a consistent block of time and stay accountable to show up for your morning "sit down" with yourself. It's also helpful to get your family on board with what you are doing.

My husband and kids know that I did my Morning Success Ritual in the morning and have always been supportive and respectful of it, even when my kids were young. Just think about it … carving out a pocket of 20 minutes each morning from a 24-hour day is a tiny amount of time in the scheme of things to aim for your Next-Level Goals and dreams to be met. I promise you that this daily investment pays huge dividends over time.

Once you are all set and settled into a comfortable spot, it's time to dive into the three simple parts that I call the 3 C's.

The 3 C's:

Clear (mental clutter)

Connect (with self)

Claim (your day)

Clear

The first piece to attend to in your morning success ritual begins with clearing your mind. You may be used to operating on full throttle with a schedule packed so tightly that you can barely hang in there to make it all happen. It often feels like there isn't room for one more thing, which leaves your Next-Level Life to languish on a dusty shelf, waiting to be picked up again (hopefully).

Mental clutter is the collection of looping thoughts, which can be a mix of concerns about your career, worries about your child who isn't acting like himself, an unexpected health scare, or a large bill to be paid. With a stressful schedule and a mind full of mental clutter, it is no wonder we are often tired and frustrated before our day begins!

Our brain operates much like a computer. If you have multiple programs and apps open all at the same time, your computer will drag and run slow, and it sometimes crashes. All of this input can cause us to crash, too, when we have too much going on at once.

A great antidote to having too many "open programs" running in your own brain is to clear your mental desktop. The first thing to do when you sit down for your morning 20 minutes is to take a few minutes to jot down all the random bits of ideas and thoughts that come to mind. This "dumping" technique is an effective way to get your random thoughts, ideas, worries, etc., out of your headspace and release what is clogging up your attention and focus. Your daily dump of clutter will run the gamut, anything from "It's time to make an oil change appointment," "Call my brother," to "I should come up with the name for my new program." It's fine. Just let whatever is floating around on the surface of your mind have a place to land. Don't edit the list or get caught up by it. It's truly an exercise of letting it go for now.

The beauty of this technique is that it clears the path for connection to our voice, not just the litany of obligations that run in our minds. From a clear mind, it is easier to zoom in on what is most important. From here, we can align our priority goals and determine our actions for the day ahead. I like to think of this process as a parking lot, where you get to temporarily park these concerns so you can connect more closely with yourself and claim your day.

In your journal, write down your mental clutter. Go ahead and try it now!

Clear the clutter

_____

_____

_____

_____

_____

_____

Connect

Now that you have cleared the clutter, the next portion of the Morning Success Ritual will connect you more closely with yourself.

Once you clear up some mental bandwidth, it's easier to hear yourself! There is so much value in sitting still for a few minutes to just BE. What are the best ways to do this? For some of us, it might be pure silence, meditation, prayers, a breathing technique, reading an inspirational book, or chanting.

If you are new to spending this kind of quality time with yourself, you might want to experiment with any or all of these. Any of these tools help take us deeper into ourselves and connect with a higher aspect. Some call that God or the Universe.

The purity of what comes through when you deliberately give space for this kind of deep connection with yourself is powerful. Richard Davidson's book *Altered Traits*, a compilation of research studies on meditation, highlight numerous benefits, including greater calm, clarity, and compassion.

During your Connect, you might have a flash of insight about how to solve a problem that has been driving you crazy, or you find that you feel more inner peace, or that you feel a revitalized sense of purpose. You may observe the endless spin of thoughts in your mind and feel self-compassion. No wonder it's difficult to hear yourself when the mind is full speed ahead with worry, projection, and future tripping. How can you hear your dreams with all that noise?

Doing this connection piece **daily** accumulates personal rewards. You will discover that this gives you a boost of confidence and belief in yourself and your dreams. It also helps to open the portal to your intuition.

By sitting with yourself in quiet communion, you foster a state of receiving, allowing new insights to come to you. You've prepared the space for higher awareness. The good news is that there is a positive cumulative effect over time. Your psyche now knows you are making space for messages, and the inner communication floodgates will open. When you Connect with self, you also start to claim the desire to oversee your mind versus letting your mind rule you. You have elevated your consciousness by breaking the habits of conditioned and habitual thinking.

Claim

Now that you have a clearer mind, and are grounded and centered, let's bring in the third part of the Morning Success Ritual, Claim Your Day. This last piece of your time is devoted to answering these questions:

What are you most grateful for?
(Example: I am grateful for my partner and his ongoing support and encouragement.)

_____

_____

_____

What is your intention(s) for today?
(Example: I am on point, confident, poised, and energetic at my presentation today.)

_____

_____

_____

What are three top priority actions you commit to for today?
(Examples:

1. *Rehearse my presentation notes for 60 minutes this morning, and then for 15 minutes after lunch so I am primed for "showtime" at 1 p.m. today.*
2. *Complete and upload the health questionnaire for my new doctor by the end of day.*
3. *Spend 90 minutes working on my current research project.)*

_____

_____

_____

_____

_____

_____

Of the three actions, what is the number one item you will do first today?

(Hint: do the hardest or most important item first if you can. Everything else will be a breeze in comparison. Example: Rehearse my presentation as soon as I get to the office.)

_____

_____

_____

Additionally, the good news is that, once we establish a new positive habit with our morning routine, it has a positive effect on our mindset. By sticking to our 3 C's, you will reinforce and confirm to yourself the new identity you are becoming as you step into a Next-Level Life. This positive energy propels us forward and deepens our commitment to our morning routine, because we see the results from it. It is enormously gratifying and fulfilling to structure your day with intention and purpose as you reap the benefits of acting on your highest priorities. It's win-win all the way!

As you read this, you might feel some resistance to adding 20 minutes to your morning routine. Adding to your already full plate is a big request, but I can assure you that it is well worth some growing pains to conduct your own powerful start each day. The good news is that you don't need hours; you only need about *20 minutes* (if you have more time, great! Go for it). Your goals are ignited by telling your brain they are a primary focus and therefore so is the dream you have designed. By respecting the importance of those dream-building goals through repetition, you are keeping the dream alive.

In a study conducted by Thomas Corley, author of *Rich Habits, Daily Success Habits of Wealthy Individuals*, 44 percent of billionaires surveyed reported that they have a version of a morning ritual that allows them to get present and positively aligned each day. These high performers understand the value of starting each day with clear focus, inspiration, and intention. They use their personal morning success ritual as a tool to leverage the day ahead and to accomplish their truest priorities. Research shows that a tiny habit, such as your morning success ritual, has the potential to create remarkable results.

Twenty minutes is good, it's easy, and it's doable for most people. You might discover that you enjoy and get so much value from the morning ritual that you give yourself up to an hour before you start the day. It's all good. Conversely, you don't have to be perfect at this. You don't have to beat yourself up if it's less or more time. The majority of my clients, me included, are able to tuck in the 20 minutes consistently, but there can be a day when the necessities of life, such as a super-early-morning dentist appointment or a child with a fever, won't allow it).

Don't abandon your ritual just because you had a setback in your morning. Pick up your routine the next morning and keep it up. In order to strengthen your focus daily, you absolutely need to start at the beginning of the day to set the tone, your targets, and your mindset. If you miss the opportunity to fine-tune your mind in the morning, the day will grab you and have its way with you, leaving you tired and frustrated at the end of the day because you did a lot that was not aligned with where you ultimately want to be heading in your life. You may find you miss hitting certain goals you'd like to have tackled because this unsatisfying pattern repeats itself day after day.

This is the formula for a powerful morning routine to set you up for success each day. I recommend that you keep a dedicated notebook for your morning practice to track your 3 C's and for some extra journaling and brainstorming when you have the luxury to spend extra time in your morning practice.

My client Jackie wasn't new to self-reflective practices when we started working together. She valued the experience of taking time to connect with herself. She felt more grounded and peaceful, and found she got doses of inspiration when she meditated or journaled. Yet, she did not do these activities consistently. Sometimes, weeks would go by when Jackie didn't make any time for her journal, inspirational readings, or mediation. As a mom to three children and busy entrepreneur, she had convinced herself she did not have time to add this perceived luxury to her daily routine.

Jackie had a big, audacious dream for her Next-Level Life. Her goal was to create a never-before-done concept and pitch her treatment of a reality television show to a big network, such as Hulu or Netflix. Yet, as much as this vision lit her up, she was not making much progress up to this point. She felt creatively stuck.

I asked her: how do you think that your big project would be impacted if you gave yourself 20 minutes each morning to do the 3 C's (to clear the mental clutter, connect, and claim your day)? She wasn't sure, but she was willing to try it out. She committed a month to this new practice. Her designated spot was in her spare bedroom that had a cozy chair and nice view. She had a basket of inspirational books and her journal and pen by her side. She notified her family that she had a new morning routine, putting her partner in charge of holding the fort while she sat quietly for 20 minutes.

Within a day or so of adding this Dream Catalyst to her daily routine, she was thrilled to discover that her inspiration and motivation immediately picked up velocity. She was excited about how energized and clear she was, appreciating how it spilled into every aspect of her day and especially her Big-Dream project.

This Dream Catalyst, My 20 Minutes, is a game-changer. Committing to the Morning Success Ritual to your morning ritual is akin to drinking from the garden water hose—you'll find that you readily receive a steady stream of new ideas, inspiration, and solutions. By allotting just a few minutes to attend to the 3 C's (to clear mental clutter, connect within, and claim the top priorities of your day) you're primed for a meaningful and productive day.

Once you have established your morning practice, you can move on to the other three Dream Catalysts, and you do not have to do them in order.

Dream Catalyst Exercise 2: Find Your Mirrors

With this second catalyst, Find Your Mirrors, I encourage you to keep your eyes wide open to a variety of sources that inspire you. Points of inspiration could include individuals, groups, or companies that are wildly, happily, and successfully doing what you aspire to do. Do your research. Who is modeling the success you wish to achieve? These role models are your dream mirrors to observe, be inspired by, and emulate. When you see others role modeling or doing your "thing" in glorious technicolor, it helps to anchor in the potential that you, too, can do have this success. Your brain now has a reference point to draw upon.

The impact of role modeling is explained by science. Mirror neurons are a special class of brain cells that fire not only when an individual performs an action but also when one witnesses another's action. Our brain encodes the novel information and sources if we choose to act out the new behavior.

Italian researcher Giacomo Pizzolatto of the University of Parma and his research team studied communities of monkeys and their behavior patterns. They observed a phenomena in which, as a monkey displayed a novel behavior, the community of monkeys would observe this new behavior and then emulate the same behavior themselves, giving us the origin of the phrase, "Monkey see, monkey do." Many studies since have shown that human brain functions mirror what we see by registering and encoding an observable behavior, which then paves the way for it to be demonstrated by the individual if they choose to.

Here is an example of my own of mirror neurons in action. Once in a power yoga class, I attempted to execute a difficult posture (it wasn't pretty). I glanced up and saw a woman in the row ahead of me elegantly and powerfully assume the posture in a way that defied logic. I never dreamed that the human body could do what I witnessed this yogini do.

Seeing her effortlessly orchestrate this amazing feat instantly helped me to reframe what is possible. I couldn't replicate her mastery in that moment but seeing her do it unlocked the potential in me. Had I not seen an actual demonstration of what was possible, I might have continued with a narrow perspective of what my own body could execute. Over time, I was able to also unfurl my body from the ground up into a full-fledged Bird of Paradise posture—strong, steady, and graceful. What a thrill it is to exceed your own expectations!

Curating a set of inspiring role models is not only fun to do, but it also serves to upgrade your operating system. By witnessing your role models, you are actively encoding new data points about what is possible. You expand your beliefs about your personal potential. You see that others have accomplished your dream. So, why not you? If they can do it, so can you! Your belief expands to hold the dream in a bigger way.

Pay attention to other people who are interesting to you. Follow your curiosity. If you become aware of someone's extraordinary life or exceptional accomplishments, take note! This is a direct clue that you have some level of resonance with them. Bookmark their website, follow them on social media so you can tap into their positive influence and witness their wins. A couple of my clients have used this tip and created a second Instagram page that is a collection of these highly inspirational people.

My client Jessie, who is a rising-star stylist, used this Find Your Mirrors approach to give her Next-Level Life aspirations a place to get fueled. Her private account is an ongoing collection of designers, creatives, stylists, artists, and other chic individuals and business owners who represent various aspects of her dream. All it takes for Jessie to inhale the perfume of inspiration is to peek at her Instagram feed, which lifts her "mojo" or mood every single time. She told me, "When I see others living their dream lives, it reinforces the belief that I can too!"

Your role models are "mirroring" an unrealized aspect of yourself. Pay attention to when this happens. It speaks volumes about what you want for yourself. Sometimes, it is a direct match. They are doing the exact "thing" you want to do, or you might be attracted to a person who has done something you never dreamed of doing, but now it's all you can think about! Congratulations! You just got expanded! Now that you can see what is possible, you've unlocked the key to potential within yourself.

One of my clients, Natalia, who had a successful six-figure career with plenty of perks but was no longer fulfilled by it, shared her secret dream with me. Her dream? Natalia desired to travel the world and document nature's beauty with her camera. At the time, she found this to be implausible. She saw no way she could conjure this kind of lifestyle. She couldn't connect the dots as to how this could come to pass. She just knew that she loved to go to art exhibits and travel the world.

In a coaching session, I asked Natalia: How can you lean into your photography more than you are doing currently? She decided to take that question on as her homework for the week. Soon, her RAS (the reticular activating system, which is the function of your brain that will help spotlight those people, places, and things that are in alignment with a focus that you have) brought to her attention a local art exhibit where she could enter selections of her photography to be considered for inclusion.

Natalia was shocked when some of her pieces were chosen to be part of the exhibit. This bolstered her confidence, and she began to meet other artists who modeled what was possible, sparking her own creative genius. This new community mirrored to her new ways of being and living as an artist. Over the years, she has won many accolades and awards for her stunning photography. To this day, she continues to honor her heart and travels the world. She is happily living her Next-Level Life, capturing beautiful images and selling her exquisite photography taken on her travels.

Ready to add sizzle to your dream? Here's how ...

Find Your Mirrors Exercise

Who are role models that inspire you? (*They are living proof of "living a dream" that you have. You resonate with certain aspects of their life, projects, or creative expression.*)

_____

_____

_____

Where can you connect with them to be inspired (*in-person, via Zoom meeting, social media, such as Pinterest, or Instagram private pages*)?

_____

_____

_____

Find Your Mirrors is an enjoyable exercise that you can continue to add role models to and check in on to keep your motivation and inspiration soaring. This Dream Catalyst gives you wings to fly and start taking the steps needed to become truly unstoppable.

Dream Catalyst Exercise 3: Stair-Stepping

The third catalyst is Stair-Stepping, optimizing and leveraging your actions, or implementing tiny actions that elevate you and take you closer to your dream.

When we have Big Dreams, they are often multilayered, complex, and involve other people and timing that may be out of our control. Attempting to make progress with a Big-Dream goal requires strategy and patience with the process. Because there are a lot of Next-Level Goals to meet for a dream to come true, it's not uncommon to experience resistance. Our super-sized goal may feel impossible to achieve. Luckily, you have got yourself covered because you took the time to design your Dream Blueprint.

Your blueprint is your guide and has a map of your actions and timelines. So, good news, if one of your first action steps is small, it's viable! Even the tiniest steps of all add to the momentum to take the dream forward. Stair-stepping is exactly that—to get to the top, you've got to take one step at a time. Sometimes, the steps can be large, sometimes small, but all together, they take us to where we want to go.

Decades ago, I was a broke college student, and my Next-Level Dream was to graduate from college and to work as a therapist and to live "large," to travel, to go out to restaurants and shows. At that time, in contrast, I was eating a steady diet of pizza and subs, definitely not traveling, and my entertainment was catching a movie now and then at the local dilapidated movie theatre in my college town of Oxford, Ohio.

One of my friends, Christine had Next-Level Dreams, too—to live large and enjoy the finer things in life. We were two birds of a feather. She, too, was both broke and time poor, as she was preparing to get into medical school, and it took every minute of her life it seemed.

One weekend, we decided to give ourselves a well-deserved treat and go into the big city (Cincinnati). We had a ball that day, window shopping the boutiques and department stores. We ended up having "lunch" at the most expensive restaurant in the city that had a gold elevator that took you up to the top floor and gave you a view of the Ohio River and city views. Our lunch was the bread and butter they served and iced tea, as we couldn't afford the entrees. It didn't matter; we were in our element. Both of us soaked in that moment in time, invigorated by the high-rise experience we boldly claimed for ourselves.

We had taken a teeny tiny step forward to claim our Next-Level Lives. We both knew where we were heading. We had our blueprints in place and that day took a tiny step toward what it would feel like to experience the finest the city had to offer. I'll never forget that moment in time, as we stair-stepped our way to our next level of life.

Don't write off even the smallest action steps to build momentum. My client Anthony whose Next-Level Life included being an author, couldn't seem to make writing the book happen with everything else in his life. He mapped out his Dream Blueprint to achieve this Big-Dream goal. His initial Stair-Stepping looked like this:

One of Anthony's first tiny action steps was to purchase a notebook and a substantial pen to write with. Both small purchases created a spark of joy for him, inspiring him to take the next tiny step. In other attempts to write, he would try to fit in writing at home and at work but could never get into it. He just was not able to fully concentrate because his work and home environments weren't conducive to the level of quiet that he required.

At the time, Anthony was traveling extensively for work and discovered that he had a lot of air time and hotel time that gave him the quiet he needed, and with his special notebook and pen, the writing flowed from there and his book began to take shape over time. He had to do the work; he had to keep showing up and do the writing.

The significant catalyst here was the first tiny step (notebook and pen), then the next tiny step (writing on flights and at the hotel), he stair-stepped his way forward with this writing project and completed his book. He was thrilled to accomplish this long-standing goal in a short amount of time.

Stair-stepping is the way forward. Start with one action from your blueprint that takes you toward your dream, even if it is the tiniest and may even seem insignificant action. Those tiny actions are like seeds. They hold a bit of the energy of your dream, and when you plant them, they take hold and grow.

Dream Catalyst Exercise 4: Create Your Luck

Create Your Luck teaches you how to take more control of successful outcomes by using a technique that increases your luck factor instead of leaving things to chance and wishful thinking.

It turns out that luck is a variable that we can turn up the volume on to increase the likelihood of success. One of my friends, Cheryl, once said to me, "You have the best luck of anyone I know. Things are always working out for you!" Hearing this caused me to stop and think about it.

Am I, by fate, luckier than another person? I don't think that is true. What I did come to realize is I am the type of person who will go to great lengths to achieve goals, but it's not just forcing outcomes to get what I want. Rather, I deliberately design my inner and outer environment to boost the chances for my desired outcomes.

To get the wheels in motion for creating more luck in your life, ask yourself these questions:

Do I need to relocate because it would bring me closer to my dream?

What community do I need to join?

What needs to change in my life so that I am "dream ready"?

What is one action I can take today to become "dream ready"?

By taking this action, will this take me closer to my Next-Level Life?

Well done, now you know what you can do to elevate your luck and create more opportunities and synchronicity.

Here's an example of what Creating Your Luck could look like:

Imagine you are an aspiring actress named Suzanne, and your Big Dream is to become a sought-after actress and land starring roles in blockbuster films. You currently live a comfortable life in Atlanta, Georgia. If you stay in Atlanta, you'll be missing out on all the action. To ramp up your own luck and your career goals, you decide to move to Los Angeles where the film industry is located and be close to the people, places, and opportunities that will bring you closer to your dream. To dial up your luck, you'll pack your bags pronto and, once there, audition your heart out and hang out at the coffee shops near Universal Studios!

To increase your own chances of success, you'll want to be sure that you insert yourself into the scenarios that you want to be part of.

Another way to get luckier is to pay attention to your mindset. Are you a person who has positive expectations? It matters. Studies have shown that a positive expectancy helps to shape a more positive outcome. For our actress friend Suzanne, who made the leap and relocated to LA and who is now up for multiple auditions each week, how lucky will she be? A way for Suzanne to upgrade her luck is to pay close attention to how she thinks, feels, and speaks about her auditions. When she frames each of her audition experiences optimistically, her chances for a good result are increased.

Henry Ford's quote is on point about the importance of mindset to your success: "If you think you can, if you think you can't, you are probably right!"

It is up to us, not to chance. There is a science to luck! You can create your own luck by being more intentional about how you think, whom you associate with, where you live, and the choices you make. Align your life to be compatible with where you are going. It is within your reach to amplify the odds of attracting more good fortune into your life. Just be more conscious of what you choose!

Igniting Your Dream—Activating all the Catalysts

Let's look at the Big Dream for Suzanne using all the Dream Catalyst tools:

First, she begins each day with My 20 Minutes, and once she's cleared her mental clutter, which includes a lot of doubt in making the move from less than positive friends or family, she connects to her dream with a visualization. Suzanne envisions that she delivers a brilliant performance at an important audition and sees herself getting the gig! She writes down her intentions in her journal:

I am a great actress and have a fabulous career in the movie industry.

She also takes the action to further ignite her dreams by affirming:

I land a plum role this week.

The perfect role for me is on its way to me.

What I want, wants me.

She places them front and center on her computer screen. Not only that, she also adds fuel to the fire of her dreams by mirroring. She checks in on her favorite inspirational role models that she's curated in her Instagram feed, just a few minutes of "feeding" herself the proof that actresses who have "made it" gives her a lift to her energy.

She's learned that her brain will take in whatever is fed to it, so she takes advantage of this fact by feeding her brain herself precisely what she wants to happen. To land an audition, her Next-Level Goal is to move to LA. She decides to energize her action plan by using Stair-Stepping and books a flight to LA for next week. She arranges to stay with a friend who lives near Hollywood. While there, she is committed to go to as many auditions as she can, visit the iconic Walk of Fame, and bask in the aura of being in her "town." With her success affirmations, mirroring, and stair-stepping, she has activated the tool of Create Your Luck by generating a positive expectancy about her successful future as an actress. Her weekend trip to LA is a taste of her Next-Level Life. This woman is on fire! By using these tools, she's kindled significant progress and positive energy as she leaps into her new future.

Listen to Your Intuition

I am a firm believer of following your intuition when you are igniting your dream. By having all your Dream Catalysts up and running, you have created space for your intuition to come "online."

Silence is fertile ground for insights. The trouble is that we often think we're too busy to squeeze in time for quiet, but this is literally where your gold is.

When you receive these intuitive hits, do you trust it? This is a worthwhile practice to cultivate, as our intuition can help us access a high level of awareness or nudge to call that person, or buy that plane ticket, or attend that workshop. Our linear and logical mind might dismiss these ideas because of practical reasons, money, or time, etc. Then, sadly, an amazing opportunity is then lost. Being receptive to your intuitive hits will add to your luck quotient resulting in more synchronicities, lucky breaks, chance meetings with the perfect person, and so on ...

Adapting this positive intuitive mindset will dial up your luck once again. You'll stay in the game and not get stuck sitting in the bleachers, watching others live what you desire in your heart.

Igniting your dream daily may not always feel like that is what you are doing, but I can assure you that you are building, brick by brick, the path to your Big Dream. That said, as we know, nothing is perfect when going after a Big Dream. Roadblocks will present themselves, and you need strategies to not get derailed.

Next, we'll explore what to do if your well-laid plan suddenly goes sideways by an unforeseen event that requires your time and attention, or you discover that you've got some secret self-saboteurs that, up to now, were hiding in the background. You might be facing imposter syndrome, which whispers, "You aren't ready for something this big," or your confidence takes a nosedive, self-doubt creeps in, and suddenly your motivation disappears. These are normal bumps in the road as one ascends to higher altitude. Have faith. I can assure you that your dream at this point is bigger than your fears, as I will equip you with the tools to overcome whatever barriers come your way. We'll explore how to handle Dream Obstacles in the next chapter.

CHAPTER 9

Overcoming Dream Roadblocks

"If everything was perfect, you would never learn and you would never grow."

Beyoncé

IT'S NOT UNCOMMON TO encounter obstacles as you progress with your Next-Level Life plans. In fact, it is inevitable. It will happen. How can it not? You are doing something you have never done before in stretching for your dream. When you are confronted with a roadblock, please understand it for what it represents—a growth opportunity. Congratulations are in order! It is a sign that you have entered new territory, which will provide new challenges.

My invitation for you is to be ready and willing for these new experiences and challenges. Be receptive to all you encounter and be open to what you can learn. By embracing the roadblocks in your path, you can alchemize them into the gifts they are. The bigger the dream, the more growth you will experience. Learning is inevitable and bound to happen as you go for the gold.

At this stage of your dream building, you may be experiencing some wins, indicating to you that, yes, I am on the right path. Maybe you are, in fact, right now basking in good news such as winning tickets to Hawaii from an Instagram contest, or a totally unexpected financial windfall that is just the amount of money you need to take your business to the next level. Things are looking rosy; you can see and feel that you are going in the right direction. So, it only makes sense at this stage that you don't want to think in a negative way.

We often don't foresee the power that potential roadblocks can have on our progress. There is wisdom in recognizing that you will encounter some detours on your path to your Next-Level Life. When you are equipped with strategies and tools to navigate those detours when and if they show up gives you an inner confidence. You know that no matter what shows up, you've got this.

The common roadblocks that you may encounter on your way to your Next-Level Life are:

> **Dream Fears** - Going for your Next-Level dream is bound to rattle your comfort zone, pushing you to take novel action and feel the emotions that come with these new choices. You are hardwired to avoid feeling uncomfortable, so your knee-jerk reaction is to self-protect and shut down your progress. This does not have to be your fate!

> **Faulty Dream Beliefs** - These are the thoughts that circulate in your mind about whether you can do the "thing" you want to do. This faulty logic is an endless loop that

tells you lies about your competence, skills, and abilities. Impostor syndrome is another name for these faulty dream beliefs. These fabrications of the mind are so believable that you fall into a spell that you don't have what it takes to rise to the occasion. The good news is that faulty dream beliefs are meant to be challenged and reconstructed to inspire you, not inhibit you. I'll show you how.

Dissolve Dream Resistance - Occurrences of dream resistance can feel baffling. You are all geared up and ready to go with your Dream Blueprint plans but inexplicably, you just can't make a move. It's as if your shoes are stuck in molasses and it's impossible to act. The inner mechanism at play here is an internal conflict between your conscious self and your unconscious self. Once you are aware of this dynamic at play, you can use the tools I share in this section to release the bind and move forward.

The three roadblocks described above are sourced and transformed from within us, and I call these inner roadblocks. In contrast, the fourth obstacle is an external roadblock, which I call dream detours, are the unexpected events that occur in our lives we don't necessarily have control over, yet they can hijack our Big Dream. You can't predict how people will act, or how the economy fluctuates, or other unforeseen personal events in your life, but you can be resourceful, and use strategies to support you and stay true to your dreams.

Let's explore and get strategic about what to do when "uh-oh, out of the blue" or a roadblock or two, or more, stand in your path. First, let's look at the internal roadblocks starting with dream fears.

Roadblock #1: Dream Fears

Your Big Dream for Your Next-Level Life will provoke some of your fears. It's natural, even for those of us who claim to be fearless. Fear is the unpleasant and intense wave of emotion that you experience when you are threatened by something that you perceive to be dangerous or could possibly cause emotional or physical pain. Most people I know don't like to feel scared and uncomfortable. The automatic reaction when you experience fear is to back away from the source. You deflect fear so you don't have to feel a minute more of that discomfort. Unfortunately, this behavior sets you up to stop acting and now your dream is indefinitely on pause. The fear may seem like it's gone away, but it is still there, just below the surface of your psyche. If you don't face your fears, they hold you captive, rendering you unable to act on your heart's desire.

At the root of all the fears is the fear of change. Humans are hardwired to resist uncertainty. Your brain prefers a predictable outcome, even if it is negative!

In a study conducted in 2018 at the University College London, researchers discovered a surprising outcome. They found that participants in the study who knew for certain that they would receive a painful electrical shock were calmer than the group who was told there was a 50 percent chance of receiving the shock. Because they had this information ahead of time, even though it would be painful, they were more at ease because they knew what was coming. So, for all of us Big Dreamers, this is a bit of a conundrum because your brain is hardwired to resist change, even when you want the change!

What is your biggest fear that could hold you back on your dream?

Fear of change

Fear of failure

Fear of success

Fear of visibility

Fear of disappointing others

Fear of disapproval

Fear of abandonment—my friends or family will leave me

Fear of rejection

Fear of commitment

These are only examples. You may have a fear that isn't on this list. Whatever your fear or fears are, there is an effective way to move through them with this three-part release technique. It starts first with naming your fear, dissolving the fear, and then taking inspired action.

Here's a personal example of how I used this release technique:

As an introvert, I used to have an extreme fear of public speaking. In school, I would do my best to avoid any situations in which a speech was required. I was adept at finding ways to avoid any form of public speaking until I had my day of personal reckoning many years later.

I had just launched my coaching business, and it became apparent that, to successfully run the business, I had to be visible to my potential clients. To meet the goals I had for my business, presentations and workshops would be an important piece of my business model.

I was truly in a quandary. I had a dream I could speak freely and openly to audiences about my coaching which I was passionate about. Would I face my dream fear head-on, or see if I could figure out another way to shape my business model to serve clients?

Deep inside, I knew that it was time to face this fear and not be controlled or limited by it any longer. I realized that I was ready to declare my dream and shared with one of my coaching colleagues that I was ready to get over this fear and go big with my company. He cheered me on and provided me the resource, Toastmasters International, a great place to get more skilled with public speaking. I took his advice and joined a Toastmasters club in downtown Columbus, Ohio, which happened to be the oldest and most established club in the city.

The group had many long-term members from various industries who were talented and experienced speakers. I found this to be another good selling point for me to join this club, as

I'd have the opportunity to learn from the best. With this move, I ignited one of the Dream Catalysts by creating my own luck. After creating my Dream Blueprint, my first priority was to establish a thriving coaching business.

Being a member of Toastmasters was part of my new plan. In the first few months in the club, I did my best with small assignments, such as speaking roles during meetings and delivered a couple of short speeches, diligently following the Toastmaster workbook format. I was still extremely nervous, and it showed each time I opened my mouth to speak, but I was also proud that I had made this commitment to overcome my dream fear. I used the Dream Catalyst, Stair-Stepping and step by step, I gained more confidence with every speech I gave.

Fast-forward a few months into my membership in the group, I was entered into the yearly speech contest by my mentor. My mind chatter was going wild. How on earth was I going to survive a speech contest? I can't compete for crying out loud! My mentor brushed my doubts aside and told me I could do it. How I was going to pull this off was beyond me.

I began to work on my speech. I wrote it out longhand, made copious edits, memorized it, and then I practiced what seemed to be a thousand times in front of my bathroom mirror. I prayed the contest would be cancelled. I hoped for a blizzard. I wished that I could magically fast forward time and that the whole affair was all over. Nothing saved me from the reality that this contest was happening, nothing to keep me from participating unless I decided to drop out. That wasn't an option for me. I decided to practice what I teach.

A couple of days prior to the contest, I met my fear head-on. I plopped myself into a comfortable chair and used the three-step process. First, I located the sensation of fear in my body. For me, it was in my gut and in my throat. Breathing into these sensations, I felt them lessening in intensity until there wasn't anything left to feel. I had felt it completely. Tears were shed. I had more inner calm. From here, I had the awareness that "everything is here to help me." This inner message gave me measure of peace and a dose of confidence. I still felt the butterflies in in my stomach, but it was game on!

I gave my best speech, was passionate about my topic, and then it was done. Inside, I felt like I was out of my body, but I felt a relief that I had accomplished all I had mapped out to do with this Next-Level Goal. After all the competitors had finished, the winner was to be announced, and can you believe it? I won first place! All the contestants were seasoned speakers. It was quite the win.

The title of my speech? "Overcoming Obstacles." I didn't go into this contest to win first place. My goal was to survive it and to overcome the obstacle of my dream fear of public speaking. Winning the first-place plaque was the cherry on the sundae; the true triumph was overcoming the longstanding roadblock that now threatened my business success. Because of this breakthrough, I was able to go on to design and deliver my own workshops and presentations, which was part of my dream.

Let's break down some of the steps I took. **The first step was to name the dream fear.** Instead of avoiding it and trying to brush the feeling away, go ahead and tell the truth.

Here's an example based on the story I shared:

My Big Dream:
To be a speaker, workshop leader, and facilitator.
My biggest fear:
Public speaking

Now it's your turn:

My Big Dream is:

_____

_____

_____

My biggest dream fear is:

_____

_____

_____

Explore what the dream fear is. (*For example, what is the worst-case scenario if your feared "thing" came true?*)

The best way to overcome fear is to embrace it. Emotions are a normal part of our human experience. We've been conditioned to think that emotions are either positive or negative. If you label an emotion as negative, therefore it is "bad," you avoid feeling it. The truth is that emotions are just that—a feeling that runs through us. Emotions are energy in motion. If you allow yourself to fully feel what you are feeling, the intensity of the sensation of the emotion becomes less. You are no longer in the grip of the emotion.

As you learn to feel your feelings consistently, the intense emotions you've stockpiled can begin to dissipate. This is the opposite of what most people do, and that is to push away the emotion, to deny it or find a distraction. You quickly brush your tears away and tell yourself and others, "Don't cry." This is counterproductive because this habit perpetuates by keeping the emotion alive within you.

Your emotions can feel inconvenient. You just want to get on with our lives. The reality is that the emotions that you have not been processed or released don't go away on their own. They accumulate within you. When you stack up your emotions in this way, the stress and tension of unfelt energy can lead to physical and emotional manifestations. It's also a huge blocker to your goals. Our Big Dreams require us to show up and do hard things. As Glennon Doyle, author of *Untamed*, says, "We CAN do hard things." I agree!

The next step in this process is an experiential exercise called Feel the Fear, which is a simple yet powerful way to incorporate your physical and emotional self with your dream journey.

Here's how to do it:

Sit in a comfortable chair in a quiet space and close your eyes, allowing yourself to breathe and feel where you feel that sensation of fear within your body. Take a few minutes to become still and present with yourself. Localize where you feel a sensation of the fear in your body.

You'll notice that there is a part of your body that is drawing your attention. The sensation can be anywhere in your body. It might feel dense, or tense, or tight. There is no wrong or right way to experience it.

Stay present in your body, stay out of the mind. You don't have to analyze the fear or try to make it go away. Rather, just simply be with it, continue to bring compassionate attention to that sensation, and breathe into it. Stay with it, continuing to breathe into that sensation, staying out of your linear mind and simply staying present to what you are feeling. Within a minute or two, you will likely notice that the intense emotion of fear that was gripping you has now lessened, as if it is melting away.

Stay present to this sensation of emotion until it disappears completely. The energetic clearing makes way for fresh insights. You might receive a download of wisdom, or an insight, or an idea about what you could do next. Congratulations! You've just broken through the pattern of stuffing emotions!

My client Elise is an example of this in practice. She had a huge vision for her Next-Level Life. Her audacious dream was to create a profitable coaching empire that included exclusive high-end masterminds in luxury venues. Elise was clear on her vision and designed her Dream Blueprint. Everything was all laid out for her, yet she was stuck. She felt paralyzed. As much as she wanted to move forward, she couldn't act toward this dream.

She was afraid to fail. She had lofty money goals that, deep down, she was afraid she couldn't achieve.

In a coaching session, I asked Elise if she was open to shifting this. She was ready, willing, and open to experience the Feel the Fear exercise. I invited Elise to close her eyes, get settled and comfortable in her chair, and place attention to where her body was "speaking" to her. I asked her to notice where fear of failure was located in her body.

She was able to quickly locate the sensation of tightness in her abdomen area. There was no rush. There was no need to try to make it go away. Instead, it was an exercise of allowing. To continue breathing into it. Respecting that it was there for a reason.

The sensation intensified at first for Elise, and then it gradually began to lighten up. The tightness and intensity began to dissolve away until there literally was not any more for her to feel.

As this shift was happening, Elise had a breakthrough. She said she felt more freedom of choice now, and she had the awareness that her past was not her future.

Elise had been brought up with many limiting beliefs about money. By releasing the hold of the stuck energy in her body, she was able to release the money chains from her past, which included outdated ideas about her capacity and worth. From here, Elise was mobilized in her efforts and went on to lead her first of many live events and high-end mastermind programs.

The third step, Take Action, is the antidote to fear. Once you have cleared the fear from your physical and emotional body, it's time to take action. Even the tiniest step will help bust through the hold the fear has on you.

Go back to your Blueprint as it is your trusty guide. What is the next step to take? It's time to take action. You've released the hold that fear had on you. It's time to move forward. Well done!

For me to overcome my speaking fears, I joined a group that was nonjudgmental, supportive, and provided a framework for me to learn how to give a good speech. In addition, I also practiced stress relieving activities with my meditation and breathing exercises.

I encourage all my clients to learn how to breathe better. Did you know that just 60 seconds, which is just a few rounds of deep breathing, has been proven to instantly put one in a state that is more receptive, focused creativity, and it reduces stress and anxiety? It's truly an instant result.

Can you identify the first step you can take today to let go of a fear that is in the way of your dream?

_____

_____

_____

Once Elise had cleared the clogged effect of unfelt emotions, specifically her fear of failure, she had energy available to act. Her runway was now clear for takeoff. Elise also utilized the Dream Catalyst strategy of Stair-Stepping, taking a tiny step forward. Her first action was to locate possible venues for her live event. She narrowed down her two favorite spots and did an in-person tour, picturing her event in vivid detail. By the end of the day, she had chosen her place, secured the date, and had a contract in her inbox. For Elise, this was huge leap forward. She was able to accomplish her dreams with determination and grace once the emotional stalemate within her was addressed.

Roadblock #2: Faulty Dream Beliefs

The next common roadblock is called Faulty Dream Beliefs, which is the collection of beliefs and assumptions that you have taken on from our early conditioning that hinders your progress with your goals. To successfully overcome this inner roadblock, you will need to become more aware of what you are saying to yourself and retrain how you speak to yourself and to others when you share your dreams.

All of us are at the mercy of our unconscious program-ming. Carl Jung famously stated, "Until you make the unconscious conscious, it will direct your life and you will call it fate."

You are influenced early in life by the experiences and mes-sages imparted to you by parents, family, and communities (school, church, and culture). As we know from neuroscience, our brain records everything that we feed it. When you have experiences in your life, you automatically make a meaning of it. Your unique interpretations become beliefs and assumptions that you hold to be true, even if they aren't factual. If circum-stances don't prompt you to revisit your beliefs, and you don't question them, those unexamined beliefs become your default. When you believe certain things about yourself and when you have experiences that "match" this belief imprint, more neu-ral pathways are created. This is why certain beliefs become ingrained and difficult to change unless you bring conscious awareness to them.

If left as is, it sets us up for a self-fulfilling prophecy, and you will find that you tend to attract similar kinds of people or sit-uations, even if they are not what you truly wish to experience. If I believe that money is hard to come by and it's imprinted into my neural pathways many times over, I will live my life and make choices from this viewpoint and continue to experience lack of money. If I have an imprint that all feedback is criticism and will hurt me, I will shut down any constructive feedback I receive, even if the feedback could save my business or make me a lot of money.

I invite you to notice the quality and nature of your thoughts and beliefs. It is said that we loop a cycle of 60,000 to 80,000 thoughts each day, and the vast majority are the same thoughts as the day before! It is a wise practice to pay attention to the beliefs you hold, especially regarding your dreams and goals.

Take a minute to reflect ... Are your thoughts supportive or unsupportive to what you desire to accomplish? Are you aware of the beliefs, assumptions, and stories that you have about who you are and what you are capable of?

Gina's Next-Level Life dream was to find her soulmate. As we explored her goal together, Gina shared that a few early childhood experiences locked in a perspective that people cannot be trusted. First, her father had left their family at an early age. Then, in grade school, she was publicly humiliated when a friend betrayed her confidence. In middle school, her first love dropped her one day with absolutely no explanation. Each of these events were painful and led her to conclude that people are not to be trusted.

Gina didn't want to go through this kind of devastating experience ever again and, to protect herself, she unconsciously made the decision to be as she called it, "To be like Teflon"—nothing could stick to her, meaning no one could get close to her heart and hurt her as had happened in the past.

This unconscious decision is a mechanism that did help to protect her in the moment, but when left in place without being examined, it was a huge limitation for Gina's Next-Level Life dreams.

With the belief that people cannot be trusted, it's not a surprise that it was difficult for Gina to find the partner she longed for. Through coaching, she able to get to the root of this limiting belief that "people cannot be trusted" and transform it into a healthy new belief.

Up to now, this belief kept her safe but also kept her a million miles away from the kind of relationship she truly wanted to cultivate. She bounced back and forth with dating, always resulting in feeling justified about her story that she'd never find her soulmate. Gina found that she was attracted to unavailable people who were bound to disappoint, which affirmed for her the belief that people can't be trusted.

Her core belief was faulty and was not necessarily true. Yes, it was true for her. These three individuals in her past had not displayed trustworthiness. But, as we explored it, she realized that she was doing herself a huge disservice to hold on to it. It was not a blanket truth that *everyone* in the world cannot be trusted.

In our discussion, she realized that, yes, of course, she did have people in her world that had high integrity and were trustworthy. This cracked the nut for her. Why was she holding onto a belief that was hurting her chances of meeting her soulmate?

Gina was ready to shift. Once she let the old belief go, she determined what she did to affirm new statements of intention for herself (*I attract a high-integrity partner into my life, and I deserve to love and be loved*). After this repattern, Gina felt freer and, at choice, she put her profile back up on a dating site, began to date again, and attracted the man of her dreams a year later. They recently moved in together and have plans to marry.

You unconsciously allow these kinds of beliefs to shape your decisions without much consideration of what is actually true and useful for you. You cannot create your Next-Level Life when you unconsciously drag your past along with you. There's no room for both. Unless you examine and repattern a new narrative, with thoughts and beliefs that affirm your Next-Level Life, the old thought patterns will continue to recycle and keep you stuck where you are and prevent you from taking new desired actions toward your Big Dream because the narrative in your head says:

"I am not ready yet."

"It's just not the way our family does it, so I shouldn't do it either."

"I'm not smart enough to pull this off."

"I don't have a knack for making money (and neither does anyone in my family)."

The interesting aspect of these kinds of thoughts that are roaming around in your head is that they are sneaky. You are so used to them being there, like how you get used to how the furniture in a room is set up—you get fixated with how it is and have a stuck perspective. It's hard to see it another way when you are so used to it being this way.

A way to unblock this self-sabotage is to listen to yourself and how you speak about the goals and your Big Dreams. According to the results from the KPMG Leadership Summit Report, the majority of professional women, even those with years of experience and career wins, still battle with self-doubt and lack of confidence.

A quick way to reveal what might be hanging out in your psyche is to ask yourself or have a friend ask you a few questions about your Big Dream and your Next-Level Life. Listen closely to how you answer. If you have limiters, you will hear it and catch it, or your friend will reflect it back to you. This is a great opportunity to shift your narrative to support you and your dreams.

Another way to surface limiting beliefs is to notice what shows up when you do the Clear the Clutter portion in your Morning Success Ritual. From here, you can do a deeper dive with this quick journaling exercise called Mind Your Mind to flush out old beliefs, release them, and repattern your self-talk.

Think of your biggest, most audacious version of your Next-Level Life dream, and then fill in the blank (do this until you don't have any more answers come through).

I'm not _____

I'm not _____

I'm not _____

I'm not _____

I can't _____

I can't _____

I can't _____

I can't _____

Here are a few from Gina:

> I'm not relationship material.
>
> I'm awkward.
>
> I'm not loveable.
>
> I'm not lucky when it comes to love.
>
> I'm not attractive enough.
>
> I'm doomed with relationships because of my family history.
>
> I'm always left behind; no one sticks around.
>
> I can't attract a high-integrity guy.
>
> I can't be authentic; it's too scary to be vulnerable.
>
> I can't find a mate who is my equal.
>
> I can't make time for dating apps or speed dating events.

This exercise takes some courage but is well worth doing. Go ahead and see what you are up against.

The cartoonist who created Pogo, coined this famous and funny line, "I have seen the enemy, and it is us."

Now let's do the part two of this exercise, so you can appease the inner-critic chatterbox and reframe a powerful new narrative.

Look at your "I can't" and "I won't" lists:

What is a faulty dream belief that you are willing to let go of?

_____

_____

_____

How has it protected you?

_____

_____

_____

Are you ready to let it go and transform it?

_____

_____

_____

What is your new and empowering belief statement?

_____

_____

_____

Repattern Your Language

This is the perfect time to revisit how you speak about your Next-Level Dreams and Goals. When you peek behind the curtain of your language patterns, you will discover where you hold yourself back. As a result of cultural influences, all of us have unconsciously picked up ways of speaking that once brought to the light are surprisingly determinantal to our success.

Dr. Judith Baxter, author of *The Language of Female Leadership*, reports that women are four times more likely than men to use "out of power" language, which diminishes our authority, credibility, and confidence.

Here are examples of nine common diminishing communication habits:

Not acknowledging praise and compliments (*this old thing?*).

Over apologizing (*saying I'm sorry excessively or when it is not necessary*).

Using qualifiers (*I'm not an expert, but …*).

Diminishers (*here's my two cents, for what that is worth …*).

Seeking approval (*overusing, does that make sense?*)

Making excuses (*I must do more research before I act*).

Needing more time (*I'm just not ready yet, I must practice more*).

Not ready yet (*I need to get another certification first—and this is your 10th certification*).

Non-powerful statements (*I think I am, I will try, I should, I could*).

List your top three diminishing communication habits.

_____

_____

_____

Great, now make a pledge to yourself that you will change how you communicate, especially when it comes to your Big Dreams. Actively replace how you verbalize your thoughts with empowering and positive language. It is essential to become aware and take ownership of how you speak to yourself and how you communicate to others. This can be a little tricky, as you are so accustomed to the story you tell!

Habits of speech can be hard to break. The good news is that you have taken the first step by identifying your speech habits. This allows you to interrupt the pattern of automatically falling into apologizing or seeking approval (or whatever your top pattens are). Become ruthless in cleaning up how you communicate as it makes all the difference in the speed and ease in which you can manifest your desires.

Roadblock #3: Dissolve Dream Resistance

Dream Resistance is the phenomenon of having a Big Dream yet putting your foot on and off the brake resulting in a standstill. In this scenario, you entertain your big, shiny idea in your imagination, yet deflect to act on it. You feel like you are stuck in a perpetual holding pattern.

Resistance to the dream can be unconscious and is often rooted in fear. Resistance to change is not uncommon. When you embark on a new venture (even though you say you want the change), it's challenging to change, and you cope by with resistance.

What is at play here is that there is a part of you that is excited about your dream and another part of you is scared or feels unworthy of this lofty goal. These two parts are polarized and keep you waffling back and forth unable to move forward. This inner tension is challenging to manage. You feel like you are being pulled in two directions. The critical part of you has a voice that is usually stronger and louder than the voice of the dreamer.

Regardless of how your resistance to your dream appears, there is an antidote to override the self-protection mechanism of resistance and get into the flow of action to your Next-Level Life. The first step is to identify the root of the resistance and the second step is to act.

Shine Light on Your Resistance

Go back to what you identified as a Dream Fear. If it is a belief about your ability to execute, and you have done the emotional work, ask: is that really true?

The likelihood is no, and you can think of a time (or times) that you had a personal success or even multiple success. If you can't think of your own success, is there a role model in the world at large that has had success with the goal you are after?

Any of this information is proof that it is possible to succeed. You are perfectly capable, even if you are attempting a goal that you have never done before.

You have cleared the limiting belief using the previous exercise, but you may be holding on to the old story. You carry a burden that is just not true.

When you challenge your beliefs, we look them straight in the eye. Your history of being brave and taking the leap to try something new is significant. Let the truth of your inner strength be highlighted by taking stock and document evidence of your past successes. This exercise gives you the opportunity to neutralize an old narrative with a new positive spin, such as, "I have done this before and well."

Shine the Light Exercise

Identify the two parts of you regarding your Big Dream: (*The part of you that is inspired about your dream, and the part that is critical of it.*)

_____

_____

_____

1. Challenge the critical narrative by asking is this 100 percent true? (Yes or No) If no, write down your evidence. (*Hint: it is almost impossible for it to 100 percent true! You have either had previous success or you have a successful role model. This evidence proves it is possible*).

_____

_____

_____

2. Shift and choose a new and empowering narrative such as:
   I can achieve this!
   I am resilient.
   I have lots of experience from my past that will support this new goal.
   I am tenacious.
   I've been courageous in my past and will be now!
   I have a great support team.

_____

_____

_____

Take Inspired Action

Then, with this new lens, evaluate what action step you can take for further momentum on your dream. For example, Jen lived in Denver, Colorado, a dog-friendly city. Her Next-Level Dream was to be her own boss and, with her love for animals, decided to open a deluxe pet grooming business. Jen's inner resistance waged a silent battle within as she stalled out on acting toward her dream. The mental loop circulating in her mind, was, "I can't succeed with this business concept because there is too much competition in my city." When she took pause to reexamine this thought, she had a light bulb moment.

The truth was that Jen had several examples in her life in which she had thrived in competition. By acknowledging this, she was able to claim this dream and break free from the limiting belief of, "There's too much competition, so I can't succeed." Now unencumbered, Jen was inspired and motivated to take a series of actions, which included looking for a dog-friendly space to lease, visiting local dog parks, and meeting potential clients.

My invitation to you is to become aware of your own holding patterns, as they may relate to the realization of your dream and to consciously choose to disrupt them.

Ask yourself: What is the *one* action that, if I did it, it would be optimal to move my dream forward. Trust me; most people I have asked this question to know exactly what they need to do!

Write it down:

_____

_____

_____

Well done! You have bravely faced your own inner roadblocks with tools you can use again and again when your fears, limiting beliefs, or inner resistance show up. Now let's explore what to do when Roadblock #4, Dream Detours occur.

Roadblock #4: Dream Detours

Dream Detours involve circumstances that happen outside of our direct control. Unexpected events happen to all of us, and when they do, they can create temporary havoc with our Dream Blueprint.

Even in the best of circumstances, life has a way of surprising us with the unexpected. There are life events that you don't anticipate that can literally stop you in your tracks. The aftermath of this is a sudden and dramatic move of your attention away from your Next-Level Goals. Maybe you just discovered your house requires expensive mold remediation, or your child is going through a difficult time and requires more support, or your parent receives a serious health diagnosis. Obviously, you must rise to the occasion and deal with what has shown up.

By placing your attention elsewhere, your focus on your dream is diverted. This can be tricky, because the longer you step away from taking actions on your dream, the farther away the dream is. It can be hard to find the energy and motivation when you have to contend with an unexpected situation. You need to pull the dream back into the forefront as quickly as possible, even if you can't push the river.

Your dream doesn't have to fade away into the sunset, even if you encounter a delay you need to responsibly take care of. After I had declared my dream to move to San Diego, and even put action steps in motion, the illness of my mother, her passing, and the illness of my father paused my dream. I was exactly where I needed to be at that time.

To keep my dream alive, I used the Dream Catalyst, Stair-Stepping. I flew to San Diego for a weekend in the temporary apartment I had. I used the Dream Catalyst, Create My Own Luck by holding a positive expectation for the future.

Two of my favorite guiding thoughts are: Everything always works out, and I believe in divine timing. I also used the strategies in this chapter to release fears and anxieties, and reframed my inner dialogue as needed.

Big Dreams that are part of your authentic self will not go away, even if there is an unexpected event that intercedes. It's okay to hit the pause button and take the tiny steps you can during this time, knowing that what is meant for you will come to pass if you hold tight to your vision and are willing to do your part.

The truth is your Big Dream will change you. You cannot stay the same and have your Next-Level Life. You will have to let go of old perspectives and patterns that no longer serve you. You will be called to conquer challenges that come up as you pursue your dream. Like growing pains, this expansion may not feel so good as you go through it, but it is well worth the effort. Your personal victories are gifts and will expand who you are as you climb higher to the pinnacle of your dreams. You got this!

Now is the time to integrate. The next chapter will outline for you how to best integrate your Next-Level Life journey. Like a luxury spa day, you deserve to take a deep breath and savor all the goals achieved, and the learning and growth you have experienced. I'll share with you essential and beautiful ways to anchor and amplify your successes, with evidence-based practices of gratitude, savoring, and celebration.

CHAPTER 10

Next-Level Living

"You are the storyteller of your own life, and you can create your own legend, or not."

Isabel Allende

WHEREVER YOU ARE ON the path to reach your dreams energetically, you have already stepped into your Next-Level Life. Because you are willing to believe in your dream and because you made that decision, your life reflects that commitment. That's pretty incredible. Take a breath and acknowledge how far you have come!

As a dream whisperer for my clients and for you, dear reader, I want you to know I see you. You are an inspiration, and I applaud you for following your heart to your dreams. You set off on this journey knowing that there would many twists and turns to navigate to arrive to your Next-Level Life. It takes courage, resilience, focus, heart, integrity, and follow through to go for it. You showed up. You keep showing up and you are making it happen!

Robert Frost poetically describes how life presents us with a critical choice point in this line of his famous poem *The Road*

Not Taken; "The two roads diverged in the wood and I, I took the one less traveled and that has made all the difference."

By going through the Four Steps to create your Dream Blueprint, you have broken free from your outdated comfort zone and chose to take the path least taken ... you chose a path that is uncertain and much of it unknown yet was calling to you, and you said yes! Well done! Courageous you!

You chose the way of adventure and broke free from the constraints of comfort and predictability, and brought fresh perspective and choices to the patterns, people, and circumstances in your life. While many people allow fate to force them to change (a divorce or getting downsized, etc.), you have created your own destiny by honoring your dream. You, my brave friend, have chosen a new path.

So, how is your new Next-Level Life feeling to you?

You will find that you are in one of two camps. In fully realizing your dream, you are absolutely triumphant and can't stop pinching yourself ... *Is this really my new life?* You are over the moon with joy and enthusiasm and can't help but share your victories with anyone who will listen to you—the UPS person, the waiter, your family, your friends. You've been inspired to splash the news all over your social media. You are celebrating!

Or you are in an opposite place, and you don't feel like celebrating and are wondering, *What's up with that?* Let me reassure you that it's normal. Where you are now in your Next-Level Life feels so right, you slide right into it like a custom-fit couture dress. You don't have to feel like jumping up and down and shouting it from the rooftops because, well, you belong here.

You have arrived. It's like you were always meant to be living in Santa Fe, or be with your soulmate, or whatever delicious dream you have been evolving into. Everything feels so aligned that it feels like it has always been this way.

Nature follows divine timing. One day, the rosebud is tight and closed, and then, as if by magic, the rose suddenly pops and flowers. Just like that. Only, that is not how it goes. The rose bud will gradually, subtly, and slowly open, unfolding its delicate petals into a full bloom *in its own timing.* You don't see nature's orchestration with your naked eye unless you capture it with time elapsed photography.

Your new life resembles the transformation of the bud into the flower. It may seem that, all of a sudden (even if your dream took a long time), your dream has suddenly come true. One day, it didn't exist, but now you are there! You did it! The time it took, the orchestration of actions, events, and people that were part of your journey fade into the background. You are in "full-on, here I am" mode with your new life. You've bloomed!

You might even have a mix of both—thrilled for a few days then a feeling of normalcy kicks in. This is to be expected. As a human, you are quick to adapt to new circumstances, especially those you want.

In my own Big Dream to live near the ocean, I felt both the pure excitement of this new reality and also settled in pretty quickly, blending into the community as if I had always been there. That being said, it never gets old to me to have so many sunny days and sandy beaches close by.

You may have approached your dream and seen parts of it coming together, and you are not all the way there yet. That's okay! You acknowledge that you feel so much more alive and vibrant than before.

The time has come to fully embody the new you who has manifested this dream. I will share strategies and exercises to do just that. Successful people use these tools to stay in high-energy states of gratitude and appreciation. The three tools are Savor Your Success, Own your Success, and Celebrate Your Success. We'll also explore the exponential effect your dream has on others. Your dream is bigger than you and serves as positive catalyst. Finally, we will revisit the extraordinary potential that lies ahead in your dream portal, which is yours for the choosing. You are not the same human that you were since you embarked on your Next-Level Life journey. Your decision to uplevel your life has changed you in a myriad of ways and includes yet to be experienced dazzling opportunities. Isn't that amazing?

All the steps and actions you have taken toward your Next-Level Life have served as a catalyst for your evolution. Not only have circumstances changed, but deep inside, you have changed, too. It's really important to take pause and take in what has shifted. Doing so gives us greater appreciation for what we have and helps us to fully integrate the lessons we have learned and the joy of celebrating our wins.

My invitation to you is for you to integrate your Next-Level Life and apply a mindfulness approach to your own personal journey. Fully consider the ways in which life is different now that you have "arrived". Acknowledge the shifts that you have made, glean the lessons learned and celebrate the triumphs and joys. If you don't take the time to be present, mark the moment and assimilate you may lose track of important learnings or blessings you have received. Here are three evidence-based mindfulness practices designed to give you heightened awareness of how you have grown into the new person and life you are now living.

Savor Your Success

Your Big Dream has allowed you to evolve into the newest version of you and your Next-Level Life. As you move forward with the next level, you are rising as your dreams are rising. I encourage you to pause and savor your experiences. Savoring is the act of fully appreciating an experience. This can range from savoring an experience in the moment to anticipating or savoring something from our past.

To savor, you must slow down and become aware in the moment and take it in fully. In the book *Savoring, A New Model of Positive Experience*, psychologists Fred Bryant and Joseph Verof define savoring as the active behavior of appreciation which connects us to the positive emotions derived from that experience. Savoring the small and big wins along the way on to your Next-Level Life with mindfulness, and awareness connects you to your positive emotions.

The tool of savoring provides us with many benefits, including more happiness, increased life satisfaction, and enhanced resilience. A lot of people aren't in the habit of savoring. Many cultures influences us to "go for it" at the cost of all else. Once you achieve your target, the grind culture says keep going. While this "take no prisoners" approach can work in a short-term situation, it's not sustainable nor does this contribute to your happiness.

Your Big Dream is a powerful catalyst for your personal evolution, paving the way for you to experience more happiness and deeper fulfillment. Next-level living teaches us to respect, heed, and honor your individual "callings." As you become more proficient at this way of living, you become alert to the signals that come in your life that are tiny new glimmers of what could be in store for you. You are wiser now, more present, empowered to claim what you truly desire, and … to courageously go for it. You have also evolved your inner landscape and let go of old fears, ditched beliefs that no longer match, and rewrote your neural pathways to gain more success and positivity. These are huge accomplishments. If you take the time to reminisce about the transformation, the magic, and the hard work, you set the stage for continuous ascension.

What is a beautiful and awesome part of this process is that it delivers your Next-Level Life, and your portal of "goodness" is now open and endlessly cues up new potentials and possibilities.

Only you know what you wanted and what would make you feel fulfilled and happy. Only you know what it has taken for you to get to this next level in your life. So much has happened on this journey that others might not know or see, but by practicing savoring, you are in touch with the truth of your experience. Take the pause, do the reflections. Don't diminish yourself and the significance of your experiences. It's like climbing a mountain—once you arrive to more elevated place with your Next-Level Life, the next level will become clearer to you and so on as you keep rising to new heights in your life.

The four-step process to manifest your Next-Level Life has set the stage for you to go beyond superficial gains, and to go for what is most meaningful for you. Material possessions, awards, and money, in and of themselves, do not make one happier. Your Next-Level Life is so much more than that.

Your Dream Blueprint is the pathway for an ongoing gift of authentic happiness. You stretched yourself in the execution of your Big Dream and it was worth it. Hard things when accomplished boost our esteem, fulfillment, and energize us. This culmination of positive energy makes way for you to follow the pathway to even more good in your life.

Savor your Successes

Reminisce on your journey. What are your biggest wins?

_____

_____

_____

What are you proudest of?

_____

_____

_____

Own Your Successes

Now that you have savored the highlights of your Next-Level Life journey, it's the perfect time for you to retake the Life Check-In from Step Three. What are your scores in each of the 12 areas now after you have been on the quest for your dream? For many of my clients, and myself included, it's a powerful exercise to do. You get to see where you were a few months or even a year ago and where you are today. What is interesting about taking the pulse this way is that you get to see in black and white—the specific improvements you have made on your way to fulfilling your dream.

For example, one of my clients, Rachel, scored career as a low 2. I asked her: what would make the career category a 10? She described her desires and vividly shared what she really wanted in her work world. She decided that her number one goal was to quit the corporate world and start her own successful consulting business. Her dream was to create a business that made a significant impact for their clients and, in her words, be blissfully in charge, no more corporate hierarchy.

Rachel was a born leader, and she wanted to do it her way, so this was the main goal. We rolled up our sleeves to get this in motion.

What was fascinating about her dream, as it played out, was that several of the areas in her audit also improved. Rachel did not necessarily focus on improving her relationship with her partner, but because of what was required of her to take action on her dream to quit corporate and start her own successful consulting firm, she became more open and honest with her partner.

Her Next-Level Life Goals created challenges for them as a couple at the time. However, they navigated these new challenges together and the happy byproduct was a stronger relationship.

Every challenge Rachel faced as she moved forward became a new opportunity to respond differently, and this is how she successfully stepped into her Next-Level Life. Overall, her quality of life dramatically got better. It all started with her courage to pursue her Big Dream.

When Rachel retook the Life Check-In a year later, she was surprised and happy to see several of her scores had gotten significantly higher (even areas that she hadn't placed direct time and attention on). By comparing and contrasting where she was when she started with creating her Dream Blueprint, this exercise allowed her to own her successes of how far she had come with her goals, but also her personal growth and learning.

I never stop marveling at how this plays out for my clients. Each of your life is part of the whole. You are never living just one aspect of your life, such as our career or relationships, but rather every category is its own identity and associated goals and intentions. They all work in concert with each other. As you place attention on one area in your life, it will by osmosis affect many if not all of the other parts.

Now it's time to hit the pause button, so grab your favorite beverage, journal, and pen, and reflect on your Next-Level Life by comparing and contrasting your Life Check-In scores and journal your discoveries.

Own Your Successes

What does your previous and current Life Check-In scores reflect to you?

_____

_____

_____

How have you grown? What has shifted?

_____

_____

_____

What strengths did you use to get here?

_____

_____

_____

What obstacles did you overcome and how did you do it?

_____

_____

_____

Well done! As you live into your Next-Level Life, you can expect that you will continue to gain more insights, gratitude, and knowledge about who you are and your life's direction. I encourage you to journal those insights, including vivid night-time dreams that have messages for you.

Write additional insights here.

_____

_____

_____

Now that you are a pro at savoring and owning your successes, let's take a look at the benefits of rewards and celebrations as we continue to lean into our Next-Level Life.

Reward and Celebrate Your Success

People who live in a Next-Level Life celebrate their successes. Rewards and celebrations are not only fun, but they also make sense to incorporate in our life. When you are in a habit of rewarding progress, whether it be the tiniest success imaginable, the brain records that moment of success and fuels us to keep going. It felt good to have this self-recognition of success, as it sparks your motivation.

If you have ever house-trained a puppy, you know that rewarding the positive behavior consistently creates the template for success for your little pup. The puppy quickly makes the neural connection that doing this "behavior" outside is what gives me things that feel good, my owner shows me she's happy with me, and I also get a yummy treat. These rewards create a positive cycle for the puppy to continue to do this until it becomes the new way of being.

We are all "pups" when it comes to executing on a dream that is big, scary, and brand-new. To get the best from yourself, add in the practice of giving yourself "treats" to reward your actions.

One of the best ways to support yourself in dream building is to be aware and reward the milestones along the way *and* have a celebration of your success when you arrive.

I shared my story in Overcoming Roadblocks of facing my fear of public speaking. I had a lot of limiting beliefs and fears associated with public speaking, but I knew, to make an impact in the world as a coach and a speaker, I had to fully express myself authentically on stage. In the speaking group I joined, as I progressed through their curriculum and completed the various learning modules and gave those kinds of presentations, I rewarded myself all along the way.

After my first speech, I rewarded myself with a nice dinner out with my husband to celebrate this win. Several speeches into my speaking journey, my reward was a new pair of shoes. Why a pair of shoes? I chose shoes because shoes are one of my love languages :) and because shoes symbolized stepping forward. This reward felt like the perfect way to lock in that success. I was stepping forward, and I anchored that truth with rewards that served to remind me of my growth.

When I won a club contest, which was a huge reward, we capped off that win with another special dinner to commemorate the moment. This string of successes culminated in the ultimate reward—the freedom from fears and limiting beliefs and allowed me to fulfill my dream of creating a business where I have designed and created and led presentations, workshops, retreats, and training over the years, which has been my dream come true.

What makes using rewards and celebrations a smart strategy? Rewards work because they spark the reward circuits in the brain that release "feel-good" hormones—endorphins. When you experience the effects of neurochemicals coursing through your body, you feel so good that it reinforces the behavior that instigated this positive feeling, so you stay engaged with what you are doing. It creates a positive self-fulfilling loop of desirable behaviors.

It only makes sense to acknowledge your wins as you go toward your dream and to cap it off with a celebration when you arrive to the point of your desired achievement.

One of my clients, Sam, had a dream to create his own branded empire of online training programs. This dream was fueled by his values, to provide for his family, to create positive impact for his clients, and to have a viable revenue stream that freed him to optimize his time.

Sam went through the Four Steps, focused, and committed to his dream goal. Then, over the year, he reached his aim. To mark the moment, he hosted a party to celebrate. Family, clients, colleagues, and I, his coach, were all invited to attend and celebrate a dream come true. It was a memorable celebration that anchored and honored the journey he had been on for the previous year. What a great example of celebrating success.

Mark the Moments with Rewards and Celebrations

What are rewards to put into place in your life as you continue to achieve milestones of success in your Next-Level Life?

_____

_____

_____

How will you celebrate reaching your Big Dream?

_____

_____

_____

Now let's explore how the exponential impact your decision to live a Next-Level Life on not only you but those in your world.

The Dream Effect

Here's a news flash: It's undeniable. We are all interconnected. Our individual actions create a ripple effect. None of us are operating in a silo (even though sometimes it may feel like we are all we've got). As you set forth on your quest for your dream life, you will have people watching you, paying attention to what you are doing. They may or may not say anything to you. But rest assured, they are observing. Unbeknownst to you, you may be the positive role model for someone, you are the mirror for them. You might even be on someone's vision board, as a colleague surprised me when she told me she used me as her model for inspiration as she watched me create success with my professional coaching endeavors.

My San Diego dream had a ripple effect, too. I pursued my dream while my family sat back and watched for quite a while. No one had much input, one way or the other. But, over time, as my dream of living here materialized, my family had become activated in their own unique ways.

My husband did a major reset in his life and work choices. He created his own new chapter of life when we bought a house in Encinitas.

Our daughter, who lived in Boulder, Colorado, applied and was accepted into the highly selective University of Southern California (USC) in Los Angeles and has earned her doctorate degree. We have enjoyed having her living just up the coast from us.

Our son drove across the country with his boat in tow, met, and fell in love with a woman who lived in San Diego (yet is from our hometown. Can't make that one up!) and has forged a brand-new life near the center of San Diego with his boat docked in the marina of the San Diego Harbor. What a delight to watch him thrive in the new lifestyle and be close by. Boat rides in the Pacific Ocean have been a nice bonus, too!

Your willingness to become the person who can believe in bigger dreams not only gives back to you the fruits of your actions, but it lights the path for others to emulate. Think of your Next-Level Life as a powerful signal for others to follow their own hearts. You become a model for others to expand and give themselves permission, claim their own dreams, and live their Next-Level Life.

What a beautiful and powerful "pay it forward' act of contribution each of us gives when we heed our dreams. The exponential effect of being true to your inner callings is not only do you rise up, you become a living invitation for others to rise up too.

How has your Big Dream impacted others?

_____

_____

_____

The Dream Portal—What's Next for You?

As I mentioned in Igniting Your Dream Energetics, when you are in a high vibration, a new portal of possibilities opens. As you step more and more into your new life, you continue to expand into a whole new level of your potential. By utilizing your talents, gifts, and strengths, your life flourishes.

Positive psychologist Dr. Lynn Soots defines flourishing as the product of the pursuit and engagement of an authentic life that brings inner joy and happiness. This authentic life is created by meeting goals, being connected with our life passions, and relishing in your accomplishments. When living in your own flourishing Next-Level Life, the momentum builds, and other opportunities are called in that you never would have imagined. Your Dream Portal is now wide open. You realize even more available opportunities for you ... and a greater destiny beyond what you originally envisioned.

The gift of the adventure that you have been on is that it's just the beginning of new chapters in your life. By taking the risks, following your dream and where it took you, you have overcome and learned so much about yourself and life. Your heart is more open, your relationships are better, you experience more abundance in all areas of your life, and you have more energy available to you. You will never return to be the person you were when you picked up this book and started on the path to yourself.

What is exciting about this evolution is that the world will keep opening to you. By being present and reflecting upon what your biggest takeaways and learnings are, you have a new way of being in this world.

You opened the Portal. This Portal is the gateway to amazing and diverse life experiences, ready for you to claim what is yours.

What is waiting for you in your Portal? What glimmers of new possibilities are calling you?

_____

_____

_____

Dream It, Design It, Live It

We have come to the end of our time together for now. I have loved being your guide and confidante. My invitation to you is to stay open and be curious and attentive to your intuition. Be fierce in your inner conviction to flourish and live your most authentic life. Use your Dream Blueprint to optimize your Next-Level Life Goals. Say yes to what calls to you, try new things, sing new songs, travel to new places, read a book that is out of your genre, widen and broaden your horizons, and let yourself soar.

When it comes time (and it will come) to dream a new dream, you will have this book to come back to.

Now you have a proven way to forge ahead because you know how to make the impossible possible. It is my wish that this book serves you many times over to move through the process of your new creations and serves you to unveil the chapter of the next level of your life. In the meantime, enjoy the life you created! I would love to hear all about your dreams, goals, and your Next-Level Life!

Conclusion

"The key to manifesting begins with you."

Diana Drake Long

How the Four Steps Worked for Tara:

Tara came to coaching with a powerful desire to create her Next-Level Life. Tara's life was "storybook perfect" from the outside looking in. Highly successful, Tara is the CEO of a growing biotech company that operates four facilities with a fifth facility that was soon to open. She traveled once a year to visit elderly family members overseas, was enrolled in two certification programs, and was a potential candidate for her PhD but had been stalled for well over a year.

The overarching theme for her Next-Level Life was that she wanted to tie up loose ends (such as completing her PhD and certifications) and recalibrate her role in the company so that she could start her own consultancy practice, tend to her health, and be more available to her family.

A turning point for Tara to establish her Next-Level Life plan was sparked by the desire to have more personal freedom by working less, doing her own private consulting, and spending quality time with her newborn grandson. The accumulative stress of current life demands was taking its toll on her. But most of all, the pressure she felt inside to finalize her dissertation and be awarded her PhD was most significant to her.

Tara longed to live her dream of her Next-Level Life but was understandably overwhelmed because her busy life held her captive. She felt frustrated and was at a loss as to how to accomplish her Big Dream, even though she was closer than she gave herself credit for.

Here's how Tara used the Four-Step Formula to successfully create her Next-Level Life:

Step One: Build From Strength - Tara started with being completely candid about her current reality. She did the Life Check-In and rated all 12 areas in her life. Not surprisingly, she had low scores of satisfaction in the areas of career, family, personal growth, and health. This honest assessment emboldened Tara. She wanted those scores to become 10s. She was clearer than ever that she wanted to live her Next-Level Life and was willing to do what it would take.

Next, Tara created a list of the tolerations she was putting up with in her current life. Once she had her list, she boldly wrote down her exact wishes. It was a huge step to take. She was apprehensive, wondering if she really could accomplish it all, yet at the same time excited and inspired to begin.

Step Two: Dare to Dream Big - Tara gave herself permission to dream about what she really wanted. Once she had the clarity that her list of wishes provided her, she got busy with crafting her ideal Next-Level Life Dream. She wrote out her vision, sparing no details. Tara finally gave herself permission to claim her desires. This step can feel exhilarating. For Tara, it allowed her to ready herself to take the leap into her Next-Level Life.

Step Three: Declare Your Dream - Tara declared her newly minted Next-Level Life Dream by adding it into her journal. She also confided in her husband and with me, her coach. Tara was touched by how supportive her husband was with her Next-Level Life plans. He pledged that he would help her in any way that she needed.

This step, Declare Your Dream, requires courage. Once Tara shared the Big Dream with her husband and with me, she felt empowered, confident, and supported. Additionally, Tara had the benefit of built-in accountability with her trusted confidantes who believed in her and held her feet to the fire when she needed it.

Step Four: Be the Architect of Your Dream - Tara converted the written vision of her Next-Level Life and determined her top three Next-Level Life Goals. From here, she created a step-by-step action plan for her three Next-Level Life Goals, all easily captured on the one-page Dream Blueprint. This step required Tara to discern her top priorities. From here, she documented a sequence of action steps and established a timeline and resources needed.

Dream It, Design It, Live It

Here is a snapshot of Tara's Dream Blueprint:

1. Receive her PhD pronto.
2. Optimize and streamline business process.
3. Uplevel her health, wellness, and energy.

Once we could see what was most important to her, we rolled up our sleeves and got busy mapping it all out. We created Tara's Dream Blueprint, which included each of her top three Next-Level Goals under the umbrella of her Next-Level Life. Once completed, the Dream Blueprint allows you to see the big picture and the action steps required to achieve your Next-Level Life. While there may be a lot of steps to get to the finishing line, it's a relief to have it logically mapped out all on one piece of paper.

> Dream Blueprint for 20XX
>
> Big Dream: Receive PhD
>
> Next-Level Goals
>
> 1. PhD
> 2. Optimize business processes
> 3. Up-level health and well-being

Since Tara's first priority was her PhD, we started with it. Here's what it looked like after she broke it down into a complete, logical sequence of actions steps.

Receive PhD by December 31, 20XX

1. Complete Dissertation
   Review current thesis and peer feedback
   Conduct additional research
   Adjust thesis based on new data
   Establish weekly writing schedule/deadlines for 12 weeks
   Final edits completed weeks 12-16
2. Successfully Defend Thesis
   Prepare Answers to anticipated Questions
   Practice presentation - thesis and Q and A
3. Graduate with PhD
   Review graduation checklist
   Submit required documentation
   Plan graduation party
   Attend graduation
   Celebrate

Using the map-it-out process, Tara quickly regained her focus, clarity, energy, and motivation. You could see her change of energy in how she spoke, how she looked, and with her own self acknowledgment. She told me that, even though she still had a lot of work to be accomplished and some of it arguably difficult, she was ready, willing, and able!

By going through this process of acknowledging the weight and importance of her Next-Level Goals and getting strategic with it, Tara was able to make sense of her complex life and the various goals that were competing for her attention and giving her Big Dream of receiving her PhD the time and energy it deserved.

The Dream Blueprint allowed her to take her Next-Level Goals and action steps and put those into her calendar on a weekly basis. Tara also utilized the Dream Catalysts, including her 20 Minutes, Finding Her Mirrors, Creating Her Own Luck, and Stair-Stepping.

Was it all smooth sailing for Tara? No. She encountered a couple of dream detours, including a gnarly employee issue and the loss of one of her top and longest managers. Regardless, Tara rose to the occasion each and every time, utilizing tools from Overcoming Roadblocks. She confided in me that, through this journey, she was most proud of managing her stress by using the Feel the Fear technique to dissolve stressful emotions instead of holding on to them. This was a huge shift for her, disrupting a long-held pattern of emotional eating to deal with her stress. She also enjoyed learning how to keep her energy high by consciously including high-vibration behaviors into her daily life. She felt magnetic.

The results?

That year, Tara earned her well-deserved PhD and capped it off with a festive dinner party. She also achieved her other two Next-Level Goals that year. As the CEO, she worked with her team to facilitate a more streamlined company operational systems and processes. Her plan included a succession plan that would transfer most of her responsibilities to her son, who was next in line to assume the CEO role. Tara made significant strides in optimizing her health and well-being. The icing on the cake? Tara also completed both of her certification programs and found extra time to spend with her delightful new grandson. It was official, she had accomplished so much within a year. Tara was loving and living her Next-Level Life.

Tara's Next-Level Life was made possible by her commitment to the Dream Blueprint process. Step by step, she was able to quickly achieve the whole set of her goals within her stated timeframe. I was honored to be part of her success team, hold her accountable, and cheered her on as she crossed the finish line!

Glossary

Arrive to your Next-Level Life - To anchor in the learning, insights, and personal growth on your journey to your Next-Level Life. Using these tools will help you to process and integrate your experiences. The tools are Savor Success, Own your Success, and Celebrate Your Success.

Comfort Zone - This is the space in which we experience life as "tolerable" but not compelling. One may feel that current life choices have gone stale, or one feels stuck in a circumstance. Often, a comfort zone can appear to one's logic and to those on the outside looking in that life is good. For the person in the comfort zone, they are awakening to an internal push for something new and different. There is a feeling that change is needed.

Create Your Luck - A deliberate and conscious behavior to increase positive outcomes by cultivating an environment in which your dream can thrive and by keeping a positive expectation that you will achieve your desired outcomes or something even better.

Dream Awakening - A space of new clarity that often manifests as an uncomfortable dichotomy of speaking truth to what's not working while feeling the desire of a new dream for the Next-Level of their life.

Dream Blueprint - A living document that serves as the guide to one's Next-Level Life.

Dream Catalysts - Four evidence-based practices that ignite even higher levels of success with your Dream Blueprint.

Dream Detours - Everyone experiences unforeseen events in life that pose a threat to staying the course with our Next-Level Life plan.

Dream Energetics - To usher in more synchronicity, opportunities, resources, and support that are a match to your dream and fuel your three energy centers daily. The three energy centers are body, mind, and spirit.

Dream Fears - An underlying and often hidden fear that becomes evident when we are blocked from acting toward a dream. A tool to release this block is the Feel the Fear technique *(see the Next-Level Life Tools and Exercises for more information).*

Dream Killers - Faulty inner beliefs or a person who is directly challenging your dream with negativity, criticism, judgment, and/or doubt.

Dream Limbo - A space of internal discontent and a dream for a Next-Level Life, but with no plan confidence or support to realize them

Dream Muse - A higher force or person that provides inspiration, creativity, and ideas for one's Next-Level Life.

Dream Resistance - Resistance to change is hardwiring that we all have that is a protective mechanism to keep us safe. There is common tendency to resist change even when we desire it

Faulty Dream Beliefs - Unexamined beliefs that we have collected from our past that are barriers to making progress with our Next-Level Goals.

Find Your Mirrors - Look for and curate your own set of inspirational role models who are living some aspects of your Next-Level Life.

Fixed Mindset - Per Dr. Angela Duckworth's research, one does not have inner confidence and holds the belief that they do not have what it takes to achieve a Next-Level Goal.

Growth Mindset - Per Dr. Angela Duckworth's research, a belief in oneself and one's capacity to achieve desired success.

Holding the Tension of the Opposites - The active internal state of holding two different paths. Recognizing that you are reaching an endpoint with some aspects of your life and at the same time honoring the pull toward a Next-Level Life.

Intuition - The faculty of receiving knowledge and insights without obvious deliberation. The ways that one can receive intuition are via these pathways: auditory, visual, kinesthetic, or combination of these.

Intuition Game - To cultivate a higher awareness of one's intuition, the intuition game is a 30-day practice of tracking when you receive an intuition and how you experienced it *(see Next-Level Life Tools and Exercises for more information)*.

My 20 Minutes - A 20-minute morning success ritual that allows you to set yourself up for success each day *(see Next-Level Life Tools and Exercises for more information)*.

Next-Level Life - A calling to a new chapter in one's life. This calling speaks to your soul and is not a "I should" do this, but rather "I want and choose to do this." A Next-Level Life is rooted in the 3 truths: to live one's highest vision, to live in one's fullest expression of authenticity, and to be free to make choices that align with one's highest values.

Next-Level Life Goals or **Next-Level Goals** - The main goals that are essential components of the overarching goal of one's Next-Level life.

Next-Level Life Gateway - The opening that is created by internal nudges and messages from the Dream Muse that signifies it's time to step onto the path to a Next-Level Life.

Next-Level Life Joy or **Next-Level Joy -** Consciously including behaviors and activities in daily life that increase the frequency of personal joy. This practice correlates to more flow, attracting what one needs, and more ease in attaining desired results.

Next-Level Life Pivot Point - The recognition that now is the time to make a change that will lead to a Next-Level life.

Positive Energy Tools - The three Energy Tools used to energize our mental stamina and positive emotions are: positive expectation, the gratitude practice, and letting go *(see Next-Level Life Tools and Exercises for more information).*

Stair-Stepping -Taking tiny, deliberate actions toward your dream.

Soul Goals - These are goals that connect one's highest expression of themselves. These are goals that are meaningful, fulfilling, and aligned to your values. Soul goals are exciting and at the same time may feel impossible to achieve. Soul goals are not based on obligation or a feeling that I should, but rather are rooted in a higher calling.

The Dream Effect - The positive and exponential ripple effect that occurs when one chooses to live their Next-Level Life. Not only is one's life positively transformed, but those in our circle are also unconsciously feeling more permission to live their lives more fully and act accordingly.

The Dream Portal - As one steps into their Next-Level Life, a new portal opens with an ever-increasing set of new opportunities. The transformative process that we go through to arrive to our Next-Level Life changes who we are and uplevels our personal vibration, attracting to us higher frequency people, place, and circumstances.

The Wish List - Once tolerations have been named, there is the opportunity to establish a new benchmark. What does one truly wish for? Tolerations become the springboard for defining the elements of one's Next-Level Life.

The Three Truths - The Three Truths are: To live one's highest vision, to live in one's fullest expression of authenticity, and to be free to make choices that align with one's highest values.

Tolerations – Big or small aspects of your life that you have outgrown and are putting up with, such as keeping a job that you dislike, putting off important choices, or staying in a relationship that is no longer a fit.

Write Your Vision – Using your Wish List, one creates the highest vision they hold for their Next-Level Life and writes it down.

Next-Level Life Tools and Exercises

Chapter 1

Dream Energetics – Body, Mind and Spirit Amplifiers

Body

Is now a good time for you to explore a dietary reset? If yes, what will you do?

_____

What is a physical activity that you will implement today? (*Note how you feel after you do it. This helps anchor in these behaviors, if it feels good, we are apt to do more of that!*)

_____

_____

_____

What accountability structure will you use to implement daily exercise?

(This could look like Monday-through-Friday noon walk in the neighborhood with a friend, or sign up for weekly dance class, etc.)

_____

_____

_____

If your sleep needs improvement, what is one action you will take today?

_____

_____

_____

Mind

Positive Expectations is an energy tool that will strengthen our confidence and energize our motivation.

To add positive expectations to your toolkit so that your actions yield the best possible results, take goals that would benefit from a dose of optimism and reframe them. You can self-coach with a positive expectation (and research says if you use your own name with yourself, you get an added bump of confidence).

What goal could use more optimism?

_____

_____

_____

What can you say today about that goal? (*Include your name in that statement. Example: Kim, your presentation will be amazing. You've got this.*)

_____

_____

_____

The Gratitude Practice

Every day for at least a week, acknowledge what you are grateful for. Reflect on three good things that happened to you that day and write down what you are grateful for and why. A good time to do this is right after dinner or a few minutes before you go to sleep.

What are you grateful for and why?

1. _____

_____

_____

2. _____

_____

_____

3. _____

_____

_____

Soul
Cultivating Your Intuition

When you are working in a state of Spirit, whether it is intentional or through your everyday life, you get good ideas that are non-contestable. They show up in a myriad of ways. Some of us "see it," or get a premonition, or have a vivid dream; others hear an idea, or message; others of us are kinesthetic—we get goosebumps or waves of energy through our body when we are "onto something." The key is knowing how your intuition shows up (as a primary like an inner knowing, or a secondary which could be a dream) and learning how to evaluate and trust it. The invitation is to build our intuition muscles by paying attention to how we get our messages and have the courage to follow those pings.

How do you receive your intuition? Do you trust it? (*Do you feel confident in its guidance or are you 50/50 on the validity of the information?*)

_____

_____

_____

Nature's Gift

Another profound way to create more positive energy is by participating in nature. Science shows us that spending time in nature impacts our physical well-being, mental and emotional states, and is the perfect conduit for us to connect in a deeper way to our higher selves. Many people have some of their best epiphanies and thoughts in nature away from the phones, email, and other people's noise pollution.

Earthing is one of the safest and most natural things we can do to improve our well-being. It doesn't cost a dime, no shoes, no special equipment. Just you and the earth for a few minutes each day. It's nature's gift.

Another way to energize yourself is taking a walk in a natural environment, often called "forest bathing." This practice to be in nature is as old as time, but the specific practice originated in Japan, where it is called Shinrin-yoku (forest bathing). The research is clear, as the benefits of this direct and conscious connection with nature are numerous, including more energy, increased focus and awareness, better relationships, increased immunity, reduced stress, reduced anxiety, and the list goes on. Common sense tells us it does feel good to be outdoors, but science shows us to the great extent that this is true.

Based on what you learned here, what is your new commitment to enjoy nature?

_____

_____

_____

Chapter 3

Intuition Game

There are four main ways in which we can receive our intuition: auditory, visual, kinesthetic, and a deep knowing.

For 21 days, pay attention to and note when and how you receive intuition. Jot down your discoveries in a notebook. What we focus on helps our brain to mark the moment. After 21 days of paying attention to your intuition, what patterns did you notice? How do you receive your "hits?" Is it primary through visual, or auditory, or kinesthetic, or just plain "knowing" what you know? By marking these moments and noticing how you receive your intuition, you increase your brain's connection and recognition of intuition and how it appears to you. The more connected we are with our own intuitive signals, the more we can lean into it and trust it.

Chapter 4

Life Check-In

Exercise One from Build From Strength is where you check in on each of the twelve main areas in your life and assess ratings.

As you begin the Life Check-In exercise, I encourage you to give yourself the gift of uninterrupted time and set yourself up for success. Grab a mug of coffee or cup of tea and settle in for powerful and effective truth telling. Be sure to have a journal handy (you will want to take notes) as we move through this process.

Take the 12 aspects of your life listed below and simply reflect on each category. How do each of these areas measure up for you? For example, are you off-the-charts happy with how things are going in the money arena or is it lacking in some way? Is your physical health excellent or are there some issues that calibrate it to a lower rating?

Deliberately go through each of these categories and assess the rating you would give this part of your life today. Be straight with yourself. This is not a time to sugarcoat how you perceive this part of your life going. We want the real and raw truth. Be completely honest. Avoid excuses, justifications, or do any other analysis. Just go for the truth as you see it, clean and simple. How do each of these areas in your life measure up for you? What rating do you give each part of your life?

The results you get from doing this Life Check-In will be uniquely yours. No one has a perfect life. There always are and will be opportunities to grow. This audit helps us to see where those opportunities are.

Next to each category, rate on a scale of 1-10 (a rating of 1 would indicate you aren't experiencing fulfillment in this area of your life, and conversely a rating of a 10 would indicate that you are "rocking" this part of your life and are satisfied).

Money

Health

Career

Spirituality

Physical Environment

Fun and Adventure

Growth and Learning

Creativity

Significant Other

Family

Friendship and Community

This audit is simple to perform yet can bring up mixed emotions. Areas that you rated highly boost your mood. It feels good to acknowledge what is working well for us. Areas that you have rated lower may bring up your frustration, fears, or worry to the surface.

When you take an honest look at your life, you'll discover which areas in your life you're excelling and what parts of your life in which you feel fulfilled and happy. Again, what a wonderful confirmation. We can leave these areas be for the time being. Then there will also be areas you wouldn't rate highly, and as you score that for yourself, it brings awareness to where you've been hiding or ignoring signals that you are far from where you would want to be.

On a scale of 1-10 (1 being low and 10 being the highest level of satisfaction) let's say that you scored yourself a 6 with money. It's neither super low nor super high in terms of your happiness factor. Here is where we can do a deeper dive.

What is bothering you about the money that you make?

What doesn't work anymore for you financially that may have a few years ago?

Just as we go through developmental stages from birth to old age, our purpose and potential have growth stages. Who you were and what you were doing ten years ago, five years ago, one year ago, or last week is going to be different from today and your aspirations for tomorrow, next year and beyond. Our life is begging us to get on with it! What is the next level? This process sparks a fresh, new conversation with yourself.

Another way to do this audit is to draw a circle on a piece of paper and divide it into equal wedges as if you had a pie. Each wedge represents that section of your life, such as finances, career, love life, family, etc. Now shade in each pie wedge to the percentage of satisfaction. If you scored your finances with an 8, then shade in 80 percent of that wedge. Do this for all the pieces of your "pie." Once you have done this, you will have a visual representation of your life. If you took this pie, with its different wedges shaded in, you'd have an odd looking, irregular shape. Maybe some of your pie wedges are completely shaded in, others hardly at all; it's a mixed-up pie. Once you can identify the specific areas that you want and need to change and name the items that are not working for you to uplevel, you've got a recipe for dreaming big.

The Life Check-In exercise assists us to take our own temperature and shows us where life is stellar, where it falls short and can reveal what is missing, frustrating, painful, or where you feel bored. It also reveals where you may be doing relatively well in a particular area. Let's say you rated the friendship category as an 8. Just because it's not a 10 doesn't mean that you must take this on as one of your goals. It's simply good information to know. You get to choose what you want to focus on.

Tolerations Audit

Exercise Two from Build From Strength will guide you as you define what is not optimal and what you are tolerating.

Start by taking a frank look at your 12 ratings. Of those 12, which is the top priority for you? Second priority? Select up to three main areas for this part of the exercise. This is important. We don't want to attempt to change every single aspect of your life all at once. The best way to do this is to choose a focus and go up to a maximum of three main areas to highlight. There is not a wrong or right in terms of what you choose as your main priorities.

Make a running tolerations list for a couple of weeks, and then begin handling those tolerations one by one. The tolerations audit often begins as a daunting exercise, but I assure you the amount of energy that you will free up will astound and delight you. Start with the tiny tolerations, handle them, and you'll immediately feel the benefit of freeing up more free space in yourself. This free space equates to more viable energy that you can use toward more fulfilling goals that help to shape your Next-Level Life.

The Wish List

Exercise three transforms your tolerations into statements of intentions as you create your Wish List.

Money Tolerations

I should stop renting and invest in purchasing a home.

Transformed into

I buy my dream home.

I spend a lot of money and save or invest little.

Transformed into

I revamp my entire money management system and earn and keep more money than I ever have.

I am embarrassed about my nonexistent investment portfolio and for earning less than I should be.

Transformed into

I break the 350k mark for yearly income in my new job's paycheck. I find ways to create multiple streams of income.

Chapter 5

Write Your Vision

Use your Wish List as the prompt and brainstorm your perfect life. Ask yourself how you can put together these wishes into a next-level vision of what you want life to be like for you. Grab your journal and, with your list in hand, dust off any old, back-burner dreams and bring them to the front stage.

Write Your Vision is best done as work-in-progress writing exercise, spanning over a week of reflection, and capturing your ideas in a notebook. What is interesting about writing your vision is that you will begin to see how all of your intentions (even if they are in separate categories, such as money or relationships) have interconnections that come together in a unique way as your dream for your Next-Level Life.

In an experiment conducted in 2003 at the Cleveland Clinic led by Gueng Yue, patients were instructed to conduct imaginary workouts in their minds. After consistent practice, those individuals who practiced the visualization experienced a significant increase in muscle mass, and they hadn't done any physical exercise! The participants gained strength by using the mind. The mind believes what it is being told, and the body responds to it. The power of visualization can do wonders for your future.

So how do we take this concept of visualization and apply it to our own delicate and new vision?

1. Start with your written version of your vision and let it become your script. Close your eyes and begin to imagine your vision in vivid, colorful, and tactile detail. Infuse your mental imagery with your positive desires and emotional intensity. By deeply immersing yourself in the experience of your vision, you bring into focus the experience of having this vision as real.

2. What does it feel like? Where are you feeling in your body? Who are you with? What are they saying to you? What smells do you associate in this vision? What clothing are

you wearing? What does this success taste like? What do you notice as you play out this positive scenario in your mind's eye? Play out the full experience of your ideal scenario and pour in your positive emotions and intense desire. See yourself as you wish to be, with all the details of that ideal experience.

3. Repeat this practice of visualizing daily. Set a dedicated time and place to engage your active mind in the details of your vision. Each time you visualize your vision in an intentional place, you strengthen the neural pathways in your brain and create a secondary catalyst for change. This active thought and intentional setting will encourage subconscious thoughts that support your vision.

Dream Vision Board

What's fabulous about the vision board process is that it allows us to deliberately and consciously choose imagery that represents how we want to experience our dream goal. Collecting and placing your imagery onto a board that represents your vision inspires and motivates you to achieve the results you aspire to. Consider it the best personal marketing strategy you could be part of, and the good news is you get to choose exactly what you want.

Here's how to create your own Dream Vision Board:

1. **Gather your materials -** Buy a sturdy poster board, scissors, glue sticks, and a gigantic stack of old magazines.

2. **Light a candle and have a latte** - Turn on music you love, let your imagination and creativity express themselves. Get out of your logical mind and into your fertile creativity zone.

3. **Rules for vision boarding -** Gotcha! There are no rules! Let the images you are attracted to speak to you. Don't edit yourself or your vision. Let the images tell your new story.

4. **Use your vision statement as your guide -** Go through the magazines, scanning for imagery that conveys an aspect of your Next-Level Life. Look for images, quotes, pictures of people, expressions they wear, or keywords that describe or show aspects of your vision. Clip and continue (you can also add pictures of yourself or others to your board).

5. **Get artsy** - Once you have ample pictures, place your imagery in a pleasing way to you on the board and glue in place.

6. **Display your board -** Showcase your board in your office or bedroom, anywhere that you will see it often and daily. By looking at your finished vision board, you are feeding your subconscious mind these powerful images, bypassing our inner critic who is quick to focus on why or how something can work for us. Let your vision board serve to remind, inspire, and strengthen your neural pathways toward your Next-Level Life!

Another way to create a version of your customized vision board is utilizing Pinterest. Create a private page and begin "pinning" the images that speak to you for your vision. Both versions of the vision board can be added to as you choose, adding more depth and nuance to your visual creation of your ideal Next-Level Life Dreams.

Using both methods of visioning (practicing visualization and creating a vision board) will absolutely strengthen your dreams. Using this methodology allows you to bypass your inner critic. It is a powerful way to anchor the vision into your being so that you believe it and act on it.

I encourage all my clients to use the tool of Dream Vision Boards to build and broaden their visions. I've had the pleasure of clients sending me a picture of their incredibly diverse vision boards, and I love to use this tool at the end of the year. It's great as a solo project but also lends itself to a fun girls' night or weekend family experience.

Chapter 6

Universal Mantras

Instead of: I am so challenged with ongoing health issues.

Every day, in every way, I am getting better and better.

Instead of: I don't have that kind of money to invest.

The universe supplies all that I need to achieve this goal.

Instead of: I don't have experience or luck with organizing big projects.

I am amply supported in all that I choose to do.

Here are a few more great universal mantras:

My timing is perfect.

Everything is always working out in my favor.

What I want wants me.

I am divinely guided.

Everything is for me.

I am a magnet for abundance, health, and prosperity.

Chapter 7

Dream Blueprint

The three working parts of designing your Dream Blueprint are:

1. **Telescope Into Your Future -** This part has us going three years into the future with our Next-Level dream to capture additional information and establish timelines for

our dream. By telescoping out, we can see more clearly the pathway to our dreams (it's also a great boost to our motivation). Projecting our ideal vision into the near future provides us with important pieces of our dream, including specific goals (which are your Next-Level Goals).

2. **Plan It Out -** Once you have telescoped into your future, document your Next-Level Goals. From here, you take each Next-Level Goal and list the subgoals and the action steps associated to reach your main goals.

3. **Your Dream Blueprint -** Your Dream Blueprint is your living document and serves as your guide to your Next-Level Life. Once you've mapped it out, you will have completed and designed our own customized Dream Blueprint.

The Telescoping Exercise

What is it like for you to be you living your Next-Level Life? How does this dream appear in your actual life? The key to this exercise is to tap into your emotions of the feeling as you envision living this new life.

Write down your experience, full of excitement that this is what you are living as if it is happening RIGHT NOW.

I have also given sample answers I have seen through coaching thousands of Big Dream seekers through this process *(you can write into the space provided in the book, but as I know you will have more than one dream. I suggest you use this as a template for dreams as you have them).*

Where are you? (*Insert location of Big Dream.*)

_____

What are you doing, experiencing, and enjoying? (*This could be a new profession, state of mind, change of schedule, more financial freedom, and a fulfilling relationship.*)

_____

_____

_____

Who have you become in the past three years to achieve this dream? (*Someone who believes in themselves and trusts beyond my "to-do list" to a higher order. I am more confident. I am living with more integrity and authenticity.*)

_____

_____

_____

What obstacles did you overcome to get to this place? (*Doubt, financial fear, judgment from others, low self-worth, and unforeseen roadblocks.*)

_____

_____

_____

What did you learn about yourself? (*Resiliency and trust. Progress without perfection. Stop comparison of myself to others.*)

_____

_____

_____

What does it mean to you to have this **Big Dream** realized? (*That I get to live the way I want, and this is so important to me. It's a dream come true. I have learned so much about myself. My life is better in so many ways because I prioritized myself and honored my dream.*)

_____

_____

_____

How are you demonstrating your most important values in life? (*I stayed true to myself and that is a match to my value of integrity. I also am living my values of creativity, adventure, and community.*)

_____

_____

_____

Write down any insights you have on new goals or timelines. (*I feel more empowered to take actions on my goals.*)

_____

_____

_____

Plan It Out

Now you have the vision of your Next-Level Life fresh from your mind's eye, let's take your telescoped vision and plan it out. It is important to take your desired vision and map it out on paper so that you have a working plan.

To start the Plan It Out process, begin with the Big Dream of your Next-Level Life. For example, I named my Dream Blueprint "The San Diego Dream." Feel free to name your dream in a way that speaks to you. One of my clients called her Dream Blueprint "My Parisian Life." Another called hers "White Picket Fence" (her dream was to find her soulmate, get married, and start a family).

What is the name for your dream? Write it here:

_____

Name Your Main Goals (Next-Level Goals) (*For each one, name, define, and map out action steps and timelines. Like the specific measurements and drawings needed for a good blueprint, these Next-Level Goals are the information you need to build your ultimate creation—your Next-Level Life.*)

_____

_____

_____

Your Dream Blueprint

Once you mapped out your Next-Level Goals, you have your own customized plan of action, your Dream Blueprint. The Dream Blueprint is replicated for each of your Next-Level Goals.

Chapter 8

Dream Catalyst Exercises

My 20 Minutes

The best way to start your day is by establishing a ritual that supports your success, with the exercise that I call My 20 Minutes.

You can establish simple logistics for My 20 Minutes. First, determine your optimal environment. You need to allow for quiet and uninterrupted time for just you. Choose a quiet space that allows you to reflect without distractions, such as your office, spare room, or porch. All you will need is your journal, your calendar, and your favorite morning beverage.

It's important to set a 20-minute block of time and stay accountable to show up for your morning "sit down" with yourself. It's also helpful to get your family on board with what you are doing.

Once you are all set and settled into a comfortable spot, it's time to dive into the three simple parts of My 20 Minutes—the 3 C's: Clear (mental clutter), Connect (with self) and Claim (your day).

Clear your mental desktop by taking a few minutes to jot down in your journal all the random bits of ideas and thoughts that come to mind. Don't edit the list or get caught up by it. It's truly an exercise of letting it go for now.

Connect more closely with yourself by sitting still for a few minutes to just BE. What are the best ways to do this? For some of us, it might be pure silence, meditation, prayers, a breathing technique, reading an inspirational book, or chanting.

During your connect, you might have a flash of insight about how to solve a problem that has been driving you crazy, or you find that you feel more inner peace, or that you feel a revitalized sense of purpose. You may observe the endless spin of thoughts in your mind and feel self-compassion. No wonder it's difficult to hear ourselves when the mind is full speed ahead with worry, projection, and future tripping. How can you hear your dreams with all that noise?

Doing this connection piece **daily** accumulates personal rewards. You will discover that this gives you a boost of confidence and belief in yourself and your dreams. It also helps to open the portal to our intuition.

Claim your day. Now that you have a clearer mind, and are grounded and centered, let's bring in the third part of *My*

20 Minutes, Claim Your Day. This last piece of your time is devoted to answering these questions:

What are you most grateful for? (*Example: I am grateful for my partner and his ongoing support and encouragement.*)

_____

_____

_____

What is your intention(s) for today? (*Example: I am on point, confident, poised, and energetic at my presentation today.*)

_____

_____

_____

What are three top priority actions you commit to for today? (*Example:*

1. *Rehearse my presentation notes for 60 minutes this morning, and then for 15 minutes after lunch so I am primed for "showtime" at 1 p.m. today.*
2. *Complete and upload the health questionnaire for my new doctor by the end of day.*
3. *Spend 90 minutes working on my current research project.*)

_____

_____

_____

Of the three actions, what is the number *one* item you will do first today? (*Hint: Do the hardest or most important item first if you can. Everything else will be a breeze in comparison. Example: Rehearse my presentation as soon as I get to the office.*)

_____

_____

_____

Find Your Mirrors

Pay attention to other people who are interesting to you. Follow your curiosity. If you become aware of someone's extraordinary life or exceptional accomplishments, take note! This is a direct clue that you have some level of resonance with them. Bookmark their website, follow them on social media so you can tap into their positive influence, and witness their wins.

Who are the role models who inspire you? (*They are living proof of "living a dream" you have. You resonate with certain aspects of their life, projects, or creative expression.*)

_____

_____

_____

Where can you connect with them to be inspired? (*In person, via Zoom meeting, on social media such as Pinterest or Instagram private pages*)

_____

_____

_____

Stair-Stepping

Optimize and leverage your actions or implement tiny actions that will elevate you and take you closer to your dream.

Start with one action from your Blueprint that takes you toward your dream, even if it is the tiniest and may even seem insignificant action. Those tiny actions are like seeds. They hold a bit of the energy of your dream, and when you plant them, they take hold and grow.

Create Your Luck

Increase your luck factor instead of leaving things to chance and wishful thinking. To get the wheels in motion for creating more luck in your life, ask yourself these questions:

>Do I need to relocate because it would bring me closer to my dream?

>What community do I need to join?

What needs to change in my life so that I am "dream-ready"?

What is one action I can take today to become "dream-ready"?

By taking this action, will this take me closer to my Next-Level Life?

Well done, now you know what you can do to elevate your luck and create more opportunities and synchronicity.

Chapter 9

Overcoming Dream Roadblocks

Face Your Fear

Feel the Fear is a simple yet powerful way to incorporate your physical and emotional self with your dream journey.

Here's how to do it:

Sit in a comfortable chair in a quiet space and close your eyes, allowing yourself to breathe and feel where you feel that sensation of fear within your body. Take a few minutes to become still and present with yourself. Localize where you feel a sensation of the fear in your body.

You'll notice that there is a part of your body that is drawing your attention. The sensation can be anywhere in your body. It might feel dense, or tense, or tight. There is no wrong or right way to experience it.

Stay present in your body, stay out of the mind. You don't have to analyze the fear or try to make it go away. Rather, just simply be with it, continue to bring compassionate attention to that sensation, and breathe into it. Stay with it, continuing to breathe into that sensation, staying out of your linear mind and simply staying present to what you are feeling. Within a minute or two, you will likely notice that the intense emotion of fear that was gripping you has now lessened, as if it is melting away.

Stay present to this sensation of emotion until it disappears completely. The energetic clearing makes way for fresh insights. You might receive a download of wisdom, or an insight, or an idea about what you could do next. Congratulations! You've just broken through the pattern of stuffing emotions!

Shine the Light Exercise

1. Identify the two parts of you regarding your Big Dream. (*The part of you that is inspired about your dream, and the part that is critical of it.*)

_____

_____

_____

2. Challenge the critical narrative by asking is this 100 percent true? (*Answer yes or no. If no, write down your evidence. Hint: it is*

almost impossible for it to 100 percent true! You have either had previous success or you have a successful role model. This evidence proves it is possible.)

_____

_____

_____

3. Shift and choose a new and empowering narrative such as:

I can achieve this!

I am resilient.

I have lots of experience from my past that will support this new goal.

I am tenacious.

I've been courageous in my past and will be now!

I have a great support team.

Chapter 10

Savor your Successes

Reminisce on your journey. What are your biggest wins?

_____

_____

_____

What are you proudest of?

_____

_____

_____

Own Your Successes

What do your previous and current Life Check-In scores reflect?

_____

_____

_____

How have you grown? What has shifted?

_____

_____

_____

What strengths did you use to get here?

_____

_____

_____

What obstacles did you overcome and how did you do it?

_____

_____

_____

Reward and Celebrate Your Successes

What are rewards to put into place in your life as you continue to achieve milestones of success in your Next-Level Life?

_____

_____

_____

How will you celebrate reaching your Big Dream?

_____

_____

_____

Acknowledgements

This book is a dream come true. As it is said, it takes a village to accomplish a project such as this and bring it into the world. Here are the people in my village that I have so much gratitude, appreciation and respect for:

Thank you, Thomas Leonard, founding father of professional coaching and founder of the International Coach Federation. Meeting you changed the trajectory of my personal and professional life. Thomas, you inspired me, and I learned so much from you. I became a professional coach in the early days long before it was "mainstream". I am so glad I trusted my intuition and took the leap. It's been everything I dreamed it would be and more.

To my clients and coaching students over the years. I feel so lucky to love what I do. Thank you for your trust and contribution in my evolution as a coach, facilitator and trainer. It is such an honor.

To my book angels:
Kim O'Hara, you are a true force of nature, thank you Kim for the creative container you held for me. We took my million

ideas and wove them into chapters of book you hold in your hands. I couldn't have done it without you. I know that, because I tried!

Chrissy Das, developmental editor extraordinaire who helped me lovingly polish this book so it shines.

To my book dream team who graciously took time from their busy lives to read my manuscript .Your feedback so helpful and your endorsements brought joy to my heart and tears to my eyes. I appreciate you!

To my incredible, remarkable circle of friends and coaches who give me so much love, support, inspiration, and laughter. My life is blessed by your abiding friendship and wisdom: Teri Tsamous, France Barringer, Tiamo DiVettori, Diane DiVetorri, Christian Mickelsen, Tanya Geisler, Molly Luffy, Candace French, Carol Price, Julia Kay, Josee Brisbois, Meredith Liepelt, Julz Smith, Loci Shines Yonder, Tiffany Nicole, Paula Jurko, Pamela Dunn, Cheryl Vitols, Wanda Goggin, Beth Haggerty and for angel friend, Claudia Colgrove, who left us too soon.

Big thank you Karen Strauss and her publishing team at Hybrid Global. It was a great experience to partner with you!

Thank you to my VA, Susie Likovic. You help me make it all happen! I appreciate you.

To my parents, Ken and Erika. The love I have for you is beyond what I can write in words. I am so fortunate to have had both of you as my parents. Thank you for modeling a fierce integrity, loyalty and for always putting our family first. I love you and miss you. Not a day goes by that I don't think of you with love.

To my husband Keith Long, I won the lotto for husbands! The day I met you was the beginning of my brand-new beautiful life. You are honorable and generous and have the best sense of humor. Your unconditional love has given me wings to fly and I always come back home to you. I love you for always.

To Justin and Emma, my son and daughter. I am the luckiest mom ever. Thank you for the privilege of being your mom. I love you both and am so proud of you. The world is better because you are in it!

About the Author

As a Master Certified Coach with advanced degrees in psychology and counseling Diana weaves together years of experience, wisdom, tools, and resources to support her clients and to turn their big dreams into results.

Diana is a member of the International Coach Federation, Forbes Coaches Council, Orange County Coaches and is a Principal Coach with Hone HQ.

In addition to writing and leading events, Diana loves dancing, painting, traveling, and taking beach walks with family. Diana currently resides in Encinitas, California.

Connect with Diana at:
www.DianaLong.com
Diana@Dianalong.com
LinkedIn-@DianaLong
Instagram-@DianaDrakeLongCoaching
FB-DreamBusiness.DreamLife.DianaLong
Free Next-Level Life WorkBook - www.dianalong.com/workbook

www.ingramcontent.com/pod-product-compliance
Lightning Source LLC
Chambersburg PA
CBHW061139120626
46546CB00005B/1858